The Star of the Glossy Sky

Andrew Therriault

First Copyright © 2020 by Andrew Therriault
Second Copyright © 2025 by Andrew Therriault
All rights reserved. This book or any portion thereof
may not be reproduced or used in any manner whatsoever
without the express written permission of the publisher
except for the use of brief quotations in a book review.

Printed in the United States of America

ISBN 979-8-9941035-0-0

The Star of the Glossy Sky

I woke up to the breeze of the fan and breathed in the dense air. I rolled out of bed. The sun sat above the horizon and shone through the blinds in light streams and particles. A few moments of musing stimulated my mind, a few insights, a structure to the process.

I was in Hollywood, California. The idea of starting a book and aspiring to write more sprouted at once.

Walking along the boulevard later, I noticed the marbled stars, and engraved inside, the names of famous men and women. I turned the corner and blinked my eyes and through the corner what's that name? I walked back to my apartment and went inside.

Sat on the edge of my bed. The sound of a helicopter flying overhead waned off into the distance. I noticed the box of books that I had picked up at the store. They were all copies of my first book, or the third version of my first book, the one that four months earlier was written and finished under difficult circumstances. My mind reeled with the urge to slip into that familiar groove: writing from the desire to write, to stimulate the mind and mine from consciousness, intellect and expression. In the moment writing, and in the moment about which one is writing, I was 23, and I was different when I wrote then, eager, avid, and aspiring under a spell of distress. One was an emerging passion, and the other a developing intellect dipping into consciousness distinct from body. My mind dreamt of writing the next book, another one, and in one dream after waking up in the night I typed it. To harmonize ideas, insights, perspectives, and fill in between with a continuation of consciousness and a nice view, they might seemingly write themselves. A book might not have a plot, plan, or an outline; but it may have past tense, present tense, future tense, or any view that comes to mind, streaming out of consciousness. Because the last book only sparked some movement, and I was exploited, this book will be more of an exercise. That is, written quickly. It might be an unconventional book, or for that matter a work of art, and it will flip backward while the world and the universe expand forward with consciousness. In a multidimensional sense. I'm writing this book of my own accord. Publishing traditionally seemed almost like a dream. I will write as though in dream and try not to alter that stream of consciousness, but try to write the book as it comes out of consciousness. It might bounce from thought to thought, idea to image, syntax to diction, and so on. If it's serious, at that moment I must have been earnest. Many times, and through many moments, I wrote in pain. Alleviated, at that moment I must have felt better, and been good.

The first book that I wrote had a storyline following a serious ordeal which made the idea of writing it seem easy. I just had to write in order, chronological, and I went about it earnestly; presumably this book will be easier to write. When I think about the circumstances under which I wrote my first book, the short period between surviving and recovering from that ordeal and writing the first page, and then working and going to college full-time, it's no less a miracle that I managed everything at once after that eventful period than it was recovering from the difficulties of the ordeal and that period. I was naive; I had little experience writing, had no literary connections or help, and I tried writing what only a supreme consciousness might take on after rebirth. But through persistence, by working on something as big as that project was to me, the diligence to complete it and more developed work ethic. The desire to write came from the ardor behind my first book, the first three books or drafts, each taken on with distinct motivation. The first version was to get closure for the ordeal, to do a big project, all of it, through and through, and the second version was to improve, the third version was to further improve and refine for the credit. That progression of mind was unique, bona fide, and this one might blend originality with refinement in stream of consciousness fashion, preserving the form. It might not be perfect. Random, yes. Different, yes. With heart, yes. *Perfect*, what is perfect? Yes! I had tried repeatedly to perfect the first book, the writing, the syntax, based on the first draft, the first longform writing that I had worked on, and I will not quite do that with this book.

I had written in Hollywood in the present tense. I was not always in Los Angeles, but a part of my heart was. Before that, it was San

Diego. I grew up in the northeast United States by the ocean, and I recall winter being the longest season, the temperature being below freezing, the nor'easters and sometimes the wind, the spring, summer sun, and then the autumn, but on the west coast it's often mild, temperate, or perfect all year round and every season. As a kid, I remember being excited for the winter almost as much as for the summer, having fun in the snow a while ago. The weather has been pleasant, the sun strong, illuminating the way from San Diego to Los Angeles and beyond.

I thought about my old friend Ben who I had grown up. When he got together with his girlfriend at college, following an ordeal from which I suffered and about which I wrote my first book, I was happy for him. It seemed like whenever I tried and even when I found my groove, with writing in particular, some sort of ordeal or event arose, an injury or recovery, even going back to when I was a kid, and then those misfortunes became a motivation or factor behind endeavor. When I am onto something, an idea, insight, or endeavor, it has seemed as though consciousness expands, and the world seemingly spins forward in relative to the expansion.

I unloaded my car and brought everything up to the apartment, and the lights did not turn on, the power was off, and it did not turn on. The water and power had not been activated beforehand. Monday was a holiday, which meant that it was a long weekend, and my power could not turn on until the following Tuesday. With that, I called my cousin Kyle and asked to stay with him over the weekend at the ranch. He said of course and then went on to mention that my other cousin Kelsey was also at the ranch. They were making ravioli for dinner. I mentioned that I was going to head over after getting off the phone. It was a three-hour drive, and I stopped to get groceries in Oceanside, then made my way along the winding roads and gained elevation and went through valleys and up some mountains to the ranch in the eastern part of the county, part of a plot of land that his friend Rob owned.

Scattered along the mountain's crest were rocks, perhaps fossils, or even relics of a past civilization still present on the land then. At night the clear sky faintly illuminated the sedimentary land. Rob explained that in the sixties there had been a hippie camp on the ridge. As soon as the sun dipped behind the ridge and the stars emerged the setting seemed completely different, crisp and still, the landscape of another world. The first time in that spot, under the sun and then the stars about two months earlier, I remembered thinking at night that I had been to that almost mystical place before. Not in that spot, but in the mind and beyond the window to the universe opened. I had experienced that same sort of awe in the Grand Canyon, under the delicate arch, beside the balancing rock.

Kyle and Kelsey had craft beer, and I ate some snacks from the store. The ranch was not exactly the kind of ranch that I had in mind at first. It was a plot of land in the desert, and strategically placed in the very middle, as Kirk had said, was a single shipping container in which he lived. It was mostly just him and his dog whose name, Nebula, I had never heard before. But later I not only understood the name Nebula, looking at the night sky and its undiluted clarity, it delighted me. A nebula is an interstellar cloud of forces where new stars are nursed and perhaps develop their shine. So many stars in the sky and so incredibly vast and wonderous, and then come day, the stars are still there, in light of the blue sky, the biggest star in the sky, or the atmospheric clouds, and the expanse carries on.

Most of the time it was Kyle and Nebula at the ranch. That time, Kelsey and I were there, and then she left the next day and I stayed the night with Kyle and Nebula.

The ranch was different from where both of us grew up. It seemed almost like a different world. We grew up in opposite parts of the country but somewhat similarly, I in a coastal region near the ocean and beach, dedicating a lot of time and energy to sports, extracurricular and outdoor activities. The ranch was in a part of the country that a lot people probably never see, let alone experience. Yet Kyle was living there. He may have once lived in the desert in California when he was a young child. That may have been military, when his father was in the Marine Corps. He had been accustomed to the heat and the sun.

Sitting outside in lawn chairs by the entrance, looking down only at the ground, it almost felt like being at a beach. But it was on a mountain, the ridge sat just uphill, and the sun may have seemed even a bit closer.

The ranch was on the uppermost plot of land in that area, and looking out at the valley, nothing but the mountainous setting and the sky and the horizon could be seen. The landscape appeared otherworldly, a kind of setting like one maybe on Mars, or Venus even. The weather was hot and dry.

Inside Kyle's place, with the fans powered on high, one could cool off and refresh. There was a bed, a couch or two, a television, refrigerator, kitchen, washer and dryer, generator, solar panel, and down the hill in a separate structure was a bathroom and shower. It was the kind of place that after spending the day there, one could be there seven days later oblivious to the fact that a whole week had just elapsed. After a few canned coffees, I brightened up and sat relaxed. I had told him that one could write a book at the ranch, that its sprawling landscape might move one fluidly along a project of that magnitude, conceiving, fostering, articulating ideas throughout its creation.

He told me and with hand gestures showed me how some skyscrapers are built and how cranes build themselves to build the skyscrapers from the ground up. I thought of the designs, details, and spaces, the movement of energy, and the engineering behind those structures, the blueprints before computers, then with computers, and how those structures could be composed and built with enhanced technology after cranes and perhaps computers. The first mile-high building might not be constructed from a self-building crane, and how it could be constructed is difficult to conceive. The craftsmanship behind that project alone could lead to new discoveries, insights, inventions, and new technology developed.

Kyle, Nebula and I were inside watching the tv. There were two dinosaurs in the desert, how did mankind come into being and evolve? I wondered that, and perhaps he did too. Maybe those two dinosaurs were us, after eons of evolution, and then I began thinking of a book and writing one about two dinosaurs in the desert. A man wrote a book that won him the Nobel Prize in the middle of modern literature, and he got that credit. And that may be of greater esteem than the credit transpiring at that time.

I sat at the end of the sofa. A cool breeze blew in lightly from the right. Through a small opening in the door, I thought that I had noticed a swift movement out of the corner of my eye. There may have been a subtle shuffling noise too. A reptile or maybe a wild animal. "Kyle," I said. "I just saw something outside."

Immediately he was alert. He sprung out of bed, grabbed his flashlight and walked outside into the clear, calm night. Naturally Nebula was excited and followed him. I stayed in, sitting on the couch. A couple of weeks earlier when Kyle had his birthday party, in the morning Rob said that he had heard a woman calling out. Did anyone call back to her? I thought that if I had heard her, I heard myself calling back to her. I became engrossed by the idea of a book and no longer thought about the reptile or animal outside. There were ants, hornets and flies, and perhaps a deer might trot along during the day. But owls are of the night. And they evolved, perhaps over eons, or over the ages.

Kyle came back inside ten minutes later. "There was something," he said, closing the door behind him. "I have never seen Nebula excited like that. It was pitch black out there. I couldn't see anything. The flashlight stopped working and I had to come back inside."

Nebula nestled against me on the couch.

"Did you step on any spiders this time?" I asked.

"No." Kyle went past me on the couch. "I'm going to sleep," he said. Then he got into his bed, and I lay down on mine. The tv was on. It turned off and we went to sleep.

I learned in the morning that my power was not going to turn on until the following morning. Kyle had to head out. I planned to stay in Santa Barbara for the night. With the power out, it seemed like an opportunity to see a part of California that I had not yet experienced. Big Sur was another area that I wanted to see, and I thought that later I will try to go hiking there, or biking.

Later that morning, I set off on a little adventure to Santa Barbara, one experienced physically. I had already been on another kind of adventure, one perhaps spiritual, extending inward toward the self, and at the same time, possibly expanding outward with the universe.

Leaving the ranch, the road twisted and turned and wound down the mountainous region to lower elevations and then to the highway going through valleys and then along the coast. There was heavy traffic going up the 5 and then the 101. If one is in a rush, that can be stressful. Otherwise, it can be kind of relaxing under the sun.

Along the way I listened to an audiobook. It was a recording of a book that was written quickly. The book itself was written in a stream-of-consciousness fashion, and the man narrating the book went on incessantly, as though it was a soliloquy. The whole composition engaged me, with the sun overhead, arching west, its light glimmered on the relaxed sea.

    I arrived in Santa Barbara. I parked near the house in which I stayed that night. Rather, it was a newly renovated guest house in the backyard of a Victorian house, located right outside the heart of downtown Santa Barbara. With trees, plants, cacti, succulents, a big patio and a guesthouse in the backyard, it felt spacious for its proximity to the center of the city. I went for a walk down the main thoroughfare, State Street, I believe. The smell of the sea filled the air, the Mediterranean atmosphere, the buildings and the shops, the mountains in the backdrop. I drank coffee in a coffee shop and then ate fish for dinner. Afterward, I walked back to the house and went in the guest house for the night. The interior had been remolded, it seemed, and it had all been prepared with care. I got into bed, then went to sleep after a little while.

    The next morning, I ate breakfast shortly after sunrise under the big tree on the patio. It was an oak tree around which the patio was built, and it canopied not only the guest house but even the neighbor's house. Sun lightly streamed through between leaves and onto the patio. I finished my coffee. Then I went back along the coast to my apartment. The power was on, and I tried to settle in.

Before then, I had lived in San Diego. The city and its scenery filled me with a sense of awe and excitement. I was in San Diego for a few months, and the entire time felt almost like a dream, one relaxed and energetic in which the sun was almost always bright. And as though by the pull of the moon, feeling wired from a long write and study washed away like the tide, from the inside out to the horizon above which the sun shone. San Diego and Los Angeles are for the most part incomparable, like the sun and the moon, and which one is the sun and which the moon, I thought, may depend on the observer, even the weather, the atmospheric temperature, and not only the time of day but the time of year. The culture, though somewhat similar, seemed vastly different. The respective size sets both apart. Even each neighborhood is distinct from one another. Fashions and cultures mix with industries, scenery, settings, histories, both with a backdrop of the sea.

I had just completed my first book after writing a few drafts of it over a period of a year and a half. I was an undergraduate student then and graduated from university a week before completing the book. Those nearly happened concurrently. It was July. My copy arrived a week after graduation, and then I set off to San Diego, thrilled from completing both endeavors amid the recovery from adversity.

I had packed and loaded my car the day before, with clothes, toiletries and accessories, snacks, coffee and water. I got up at 5:00am that morning and ate breakfast and then was on the road by 6:00am.

There may be no line linear on the road less traveled, I thought. America, rich in history, progressive in development.

It must evolve into a greater domain, materially, intellectually, influenced by consciousness. Even knowledge and scholarship must evolve and the refinement of learning develop. Evolution of mind and body, of being and spirituality, must be a primary aspect of the cumulative journey.

The route to Cleveland was down the coast from Portland and through inland Massachusetts and then the plains and hills of New York. The sun, peering through spaces in the sky and gaps between clouds intermittently, cast light upon the undulating hills, forests, bodies of water, and continued to shine, from Albany to Rochester, Buffalo to Erie. There was a quick stretch through Pennsylvania, and someone in a vehicle waved through the window. I carried on, as the car fell back behind the traffic, and a couple hours later I arrived in Cleveland.

On a pier, extending out over the water from the banks of Lake Erie, there was a blonde girl with wavy hair and curls. She was with her group. And the waves came in, washing onto the deck of the pier. As the sun dipped toward the horizon, setting in the sky, hues of red appeared on clouds and throughout the surrounding landscape and the lake ahead, reflecting off the water, faintly illuminating her complexion. The waves continued to flow in. My shoes got wet. A sense of oneness emerged, and then the sun brightly set.

From Cleveland, the route was almost a continuous straight line on the highway to Des Moines. Flocks of birds soared in the sky over endless fields of crops and grains. The route went right outside of Chicago, and perhaps only glimpses of the city's architecture were caught going along the freeway, but not the mighty buildings and those of influence that progressed urban development. Following a bend and light curvature to the infrastructure, the remainder of the course that day was linear. The road stretched out to the horizon flat and straight, the sun overhead, in motion with one, as a bundle of clouds formed far off to the left in the afternoon.

I ate a rice bowl for dinner, with chicken and green vegetables, and then went to bed. Then I drank coffee in the morning, ate a light breakfast, and set off to Denver.

The first two hundred miles of Colorado going east to west had flat roads and fields and short-grass prairies on either side all the way out to the horizon. The road went through the landscape in a linear path and narrowed to the width of a line the further out it went. There was a slight incline for a way, and the hills covered in dry grass glowed under the sun. All along the drive there had been wind turbines scattered throughout the different landscapes, landforms and regions. The elevation had gained substantially. The road maybe sloped downward for some distance, as though approaching a valley, then suddenly the highway expanded, and there were more lanes, more traffic, a slight curve to the road after which the skyline of Denver entered view. The Rocky Mountains stood in the backdrop and towered over the city. Buildings and structures shone in the sunlight and almost huddled together in the valley. I stayed the night in downtown. Despite Covid-19, some historic streets with shops and restaurants were busy, but there was not much traffic. I did some exercises at night, and again in the morning. I drank coffee and had breakfast, then set off on the road, going into the mountains, winding between peaks, up and down slopes, through passes, rugged notches, valleys, and through tunnels before the landscape transitioned to soil rich in iron with unique rock formations sometimes quite complex in shape.

 Moab sat nestled at the bottom of a canyon around which its vibrant walls curved upward toward the sky. The sunset landscape expanded in all directions. Some prominent attractions were located nearby. Looking out from the top of a plateau, the little spot out there on the ground below, the eagle wonders, is it a mile away, five, or five hundred? The sun slowly dipped, and the sunset indeed appeared spectacular, complementing the red rock formations and the vast, glowing landscape. I stood next to the delicate rock and under the delicate arch. I later looked up and saw perhaps a nebula. The sky almost seemed alive, boundless and brilliant, with the light of the moon and all the stars active the expanse of the universe beyond and that of consciousness within.

 At the inn, I washed up and brushed my teeth and went to bed. I woke up before the sunrise. I drank coffee, then got on the road and started driving, with the still brilliance of the sky reflecting in the side and rear-view mirrors.

 Around almost every turn stood a geographic feature, different rock formations, as the soil transformed to the texture of sand. Each mirror displayed a different rock or formation of the landscape. A three-way feature resembling a cluster of pillars stood to the right. To the left was what looked like the colosseum. And at one point appeared to be the Red Sea parting, with the road going right along the middle of it. Some of the rocks and rock formations looked like something familiar, all different, but similar, like clouds in the sky. One formation could have been a woman, built like a cactus. The sun's radiance picked up throughout the day. I arrived in Las Vegas that afternoon and stayed in an iconic hotel along the main strip, the Bellagio. After checking in, I saw some of the attractions within the hotel, played some games in the casino, lost and won, ate dinner and then went up to my room. The bathroom was marbled. I washed up and changed into loungewear and got into bed and on the computer. A little later, I went to sleep, then woke up early, drank coffee, ate breakfast, and started on the stretch to San Diego.

From when I arrived until I started a new book, the beginning steps to this book, the notes and the mindset for a project, Pacific Beach and its setting had me in awe. Even when the sun shone on the fronds of clustered trees, the radiance of both filled the air with rapture and a sense of relaxation. Swaying in the breeze, they stood highlighted by the sun almost suggestively. One might absorb the essence of their radiance sitting before one or a cluster of many. The experience may be meditative. The contentment in pose might be seen only in the animal kingdom, such as a cat perched on a ledge, an alligator on a bank, a bird on a branch, a fly on the water of a lake. I have always thought that consciousness is part of something more than can be beheld, something greater, something real or even tangible rather than abstract. For as long as I can remember that abstraction has been like real gold, and I've always been captivated by its brilliance. Even as a kid I had an infatuation for discovering treasure, a treasure that was completely material, or even raw. It may have been an ancient treasure, such as those found in Hollywood films, gold coins and crowns, rubies and chests, scrolls and silver, or something much simpler, like ore. And then the treasure became abstract, creative ideas, revolving around cognition: creative treasure in a way, like creating a book, with byproducts of the cognitive process or one's consciousness within scattered all throughout. Just as I had once sought after and dreamed of discovering material treasure, such as those in my favorite childhood adventure films, now more than ever a book ought to be sought after and discovered even if it has within only a few creative ideas, progressive insights, or as a whole, transcend a realm. The ore comes from within, like the gold on earth, scattered within its layers, the crust, the mantle, the core. Abstractly, it can be within lines, paragraphs, pages, deep within or all throughout the collective consciousness. And yet an abstract but tangible one was right there, with the radiance of the sunset, the land meeting the sea, the fronds and leaves in the breeze.

From the very beginning, there was light. Energy flowed through landforms, like wind blowing on the crest of a hill or a mountain, through its elements, openings, orifices, or even as vibrations through the ground, along a subduction zone, forming waves. All the energy that went into completing my first book at a time of distress and diligence must have been kinetic, perhaps a force behind consciousness. To be on that part of the wave, one's balance might have to be adjusted. The arid land sloped up from the seabed, absorbing that energy like a sponge. Just down the coast sandstone cliffs and bluffs delineating the land's edge pooled below what the rock formations reflected, flowing in, and flowing out into the continuous motion of waves.

My roommate who was also the landlord gave me a quick tour of the condo, from the living room to my bedroom upstairs, the big bathroom, large closet, and connected balcony around which some potted plants grew. Later that afternoon, he gave me a bike tour of the neighborhood. I thought that it might have been one of the greatest bike rides that I had ever been on. It became an evening routine for a little while, and then that routine became a run, and I went on the run four or five nights a week. From the middle of Pacific Beach, the route looped around the southern portion of the neighborhood, starting on Hornblend and turning left down Kendall and then down to Crown Point. Moving along the path that follows the beach, there were often bonfires and parties, acrobats and artists, people putting on performances. Sometimes I slowed down to see all that was happening, or on quieter nights it was the perpetual clear sky that appeared fascinating. A bonsai tree stood between the pathway and the water of Fiesta Bay, and its stark silhouette accentuated the background and above, lights in the sky dotting the vast, dark space heavily diluted by the glow of downtown, the glow of houses on the hills of Bay Park, Point Loma, and Old Town. I ran under the bridge and climbed up the path to the bayside drive and went over and up and back to the street on which I had started running down. Turning down Hornblend, I began to cool off. Then at the condo I went up to my room and then out on the balcony. The leaves on the trees growing up from the front yard fluttered beside the banister, kind of like crinkling paper. I sat on the couch outside for a little while, and the subtle vibrations and moments of stillness fostered a brief meditation.

On the first night, after the bike ride, I sat outside on the balcony in a reverie. Nick had not only showed me what later turned into part of my run, I saw Pacific Beach from Garnet down almost in its entirety. We rode on the bike path along Mission Bay from beginning to end, and at one point, elated I imagined taking Hannah on the exact route. Nick cut through Belmont Park, and we continued down the path on Mission Beach, weaving between others walking or riding bikes. The setting seemed beautiful. I continued along the pathway. The gloom of June had extended into July, and the sun set behind a cluster of clouds as rays of light streamed down across the horizon and over the water like afternoon rain. We then crossed the street and rode our bikes along the main thoroughfare in the sun.

When I got back to the house, I went upstairs and out on the balcony. The couch sat on the floor against the far wall, all made of material that gave the whole space a Mediterranean aesthetic, with the cluster of trees growing up beside the front facade from the yard below, and some fronds drooping in and over the banister, over some pottery and patio furniture set around the floor. It could have been part of a castle, a palace, or a fortress. Against the side wall sat a patio table and two chairs. I ate my breakfast outside in the shade on occasion, a couple of eggs and half an avocado—when the avocado in me was unfermentable—and a glass of juice, lemon juice with water. There was a pomegranate tree in the front yard, growing almost directly beneath the balcony. All around were exotic pots and plants, various cacti and succulents. On a little stool beside the table was a small juniper tree, and next to that, a dehydrated cerulean. I was excited that night upon arrival.

The following day, I began checking out the area north of Garnet on a bike, going along the side of the street toward the beach. I went up a slight grade, turned the corner, pedaled lightly, calmly, almost in a reverie, and then suddenly I heard a strange noise. I looked around. I was on Emerald approaching Cass and nearing the four-way intersection. It seemed like a truck had crashed into a barbeque or had been driving with a barbeque in the bed of the truck, and then the grill fell into the middle of the intersection. At first, there was a metal thump, a clunk, a large object on the pavement, possibly smoke rising into the air. But it was not a barbeque or a grill, it was someone's motorcycle, and the driver had fallen off.

He groaned.

Fronds swaying in the wind slowed, it seemed. My stomach sank into my gut, and my heartbeat picked up.

He was in pain. Perhaps the crash had been disorienting. It evoked some memory of the trauma about which I had written in my first book and a sense of profound empathy.

I remembered being told that I was quiet, given the severity of the ordeal, though not unconsciousness. I was incoherent but somewhat responsive, I suppose, as amnesia set in. I had suffered serious injuries to the body and brain and then woke up from a week-long coma nearly three and a half years earlier to that day.

A crowd of people formed on every corner of the intersection, and then the police arrived, the first responders, followed by an ambulance and a firetruck. The motorcyclist was lifted onto a stretcher and went into the ambulance. Some people that had come out of their apartments or condos walked back inside. The motorcyclist had gone through the stop sign at the same time the truck was going through the intersection. It might have been a kind of higher intervention, I thought.

I rode my bike down the street to the right. I stopped at the end of the block next to a sunglass shop. I went inside, browsed around for a minute, looking at the sunglasses on display. Then another motorcycle went by.

Later I learned that motorcycles are somewhat popular in Pacific Beach and throughout the city. On the balcony, maybe a few times each night, the deep resonating sound of one going by filled and ripped through the air. During the day, they sped by and swerved between traffic on the freeways and at red lights. There must have been a rush, the noise and roar of a full stadium.

I had just gone quite a long way, the whole width of the continental landmass, and how exciting it had been. Upon arriving it was a bit difficult to meet others in the midst of Covid-19. Most indoor venues and businesses were closed, and there were almost no events. I did yoga in a group class outdoors. The water and the sky blended in the backdrop, vast, open and calm but energetic. One night I went to a bonfire on the beach in La Jolla.

There were some characters at that gathering. The natives were friendly, relaxed and cool. The host who organized the event had been living on a roof under the stars, he explained, and then he started hosting the group events after promoting them on social media. For most of the night I hung out around the bonfire, walked on the beach or out to the water, and then I was followed around by a few others who had arrived at the event around the time that I did. Two of them were foreign, and from what part of the world they were from, I don't remember. They talked about girls in a kind of elementary manner, as though the San Diego girls had them awestruck, it seemed. They were trying to meet a girl, but the girls came from somewhere else. Naturally, the native girls did too. One's shine from the sun and the light of the moon may be rooted in European ancestry. Some are possibly distant relatives of the land's first settlers, developers, or the world's subsequent explorers. They must have made bonfires on the beach, as that bright aesthetic evolved from climate and environment throughout the ages and each generation.

The following day, I still smelled like the bonfire, or rather I still smelled the bonfire. By chance, I had sat downwind right where the smoke was blowing, and that night the wind was persistent and gusty. If I changed my position or seat around the circle, the wind often changed direction and followed, blowing every which way. Along the beach, the light gusts under the night sky carried a sweet scent of the ocean mixed with minerals. The tide must have been going out. After a little while at the bonfire, I went back to the condo and up to bed.

The next week Kyle came into town to go shopping and to meet up. I hadn't seen him since the start of my adolescence about a decade earlier. He had lived in Pacific Beach for a while throughout his 20s. We met in the afternoon for a bite to eat at a local pizza shop. I ordered French fries and a glass of water. When Kyle lived there, he had been a nanny for a family of four at the beginning, and he told me that he used to live at their house. They sometimes ate dinner together, did activities together, and they paid him for looking after the kids. "Some of the time we played video games together," he said. "But I couldn't play violent video games in the house, or explicit ones."

"I haven't played videogames in a while," I said.

"Rated M games, mature games, were limited. We didn't play any in front of the kids, or R-rated movies."

Kyle went on a little bit about the kids and their differences from one another. They were boys, but one of the boys was born a girl. Then about a year before he had started nannying, she preferred the pronoun he.

"He switched his name," Kyle said. "I'm not sure his birth name. Nathaniel became his preferred name."

As he mentioned that, the first girl's name that I thought of was Natalia.

"His mother's little girl, Nathaniel."

"It might have been kind of young for a name change like that," I said. "Natalia to Nathaniel."

"Natalia? I don't know what Nathaniel's name was."

I ate a French fry, then drank some water.

"I think it started on Halloween. She dressed as Superman, maybe instead of Wonder Woman. Then she was dressing in her brother's clothes. Her parents thought it was a phase. But soon after that she had her own boy's clothes."

"When I was younger, I went through a movie phase and watched a lot of movies," I said.

"What movies?"

"Austin Powers."

"I thought you were into skateboarding."

"I was, and I was pretty good."

"It's Southern California," he said. "Get back into skating."

"I might try to."

"Go for it."

"Sure."

"You're into writing, right?"

"Yes, the whole process of writing and putting a book together. Endeavors like that. Starting from one line and turning it into a big project."

"Cool. Well anyway, she changed names. Was into books too. Then she started wearing boys clothing and pretty soon she was a boy. It went from costumes and clothes to Nathaniel. I learned about that while having drinks with their parents."

"That's interesting."

"I don't drink much."

"Neither do I. But I like to when I do."

"Same. It's San Diego, they said."

"Cheers." I raised my glass.

Kyle then mentioned the ranch, that he was living on a ranch in the eastern part of San Diego. "Come out to the ranch anytime. Matt is coming this weekend and for a few days next week. Kelsey's coming down Sunday. She's only a couple of hours away, near Anaheim. Matt said that he wants to go to the safari. I said sure dude, we can check it out. It's way up near Escondido. I've never been to the safari. You can come too if you want."

"I'm down," I said.

My cousins and I had got together the following week at the ranch. Matt, the youngest, flew into Los Angeles with his girlfriend the previous day and spent the night with Kelsey at her apartment. She ordered them some Italian food, a three-course meal that they all described: focaccia bread, carbonara, tortellini, and desert. We lived on opposite ends of the country growing up. I had only visited them once when I was five or maybe six years old. Or it was twice, once when I was five and again when I was six, and both times sort of blended as one. Normally we all met up at my aunt and uncle's house or else at the cottage in which my grandparents lived in the summer. In any case, I was surprised back then to discover that their lifestyles were so similar. The climate was a bit different, more humid, longer summers, milder winters, stronger storms. They had a lot of bikes, some skateboards, scooters, even a go-kart. I remember when I arrived and every house on their block was made of brick, and they were large houses, I believe less expensive than the house that I grew up in. The region that they lived in produced a lot of clay, I was told. Most of the houses where I grew up were made of wood, and there were many pine, evergreen, and deciduous trees. They had the same or similar varieties, and some were different. We rode in motorized vehicles along a wooded path and we may have popped out behind a school, or it was a public garden. I remember better our holidays and get-togethers in Virginia, and their visits to where I lived, the beach, the ice cream shops, the amusement parks.

 The ice cream—no one brought the ice cream, well great!

 My cousin did not eat ice cream then. Neither did I, for the most part. I was still trying to figure out my digestive system then, and I had been for quite a while, its distress, and ultimately the disorders behind that distress. At that time, it seemed like a puzzle, only one diligently decipherable.

 They had asked me to pick up a couple of local pies along the way to the ranch. The store was busy, and I waited in the checkout line extending out the front door and into the parking lot. Some folks in line came all the way from another continent. Kyle had mentioned that the pie was popular in San Diego, and later that the area sometimes had a lot of campers in RVs. There were some mountains and trails and extensive open space for offroad adventures, hiking, biking, stargazing. The campers sometimes left trash and waste on the side of the road, he told me. That rankled him. Tree coverage was sparse except for along the course of rivers and streams. I followed the winding roads into the mountainous region and out to the ranch under the sun.

When Kyle said that his friend's family owned a ranch, and that he was living on it at that time, I had in mind something spectacular, a grand, expansive property. Well maybe it was spectacular, in an unexpected way. But when I first thought of a ranch, I thought of a large property with an expanse of land and fields and trees, possibly animals grazing out front beside the entrance and horses drinking from a pond, and built somewhere toward the back near the property line is a grand house made of timber and stone. Driving up the sand driveway full of dips and ruts, it was a bit different than that. There was Kyle standing on top of an intermodal container, waving, welcome to the ranch.

I stayed at the ranch for a couple of days. Outside at night the winds howled across the landscape between frequent powerful gusts, blowing against the hollow steel rectangular structures and sounding almost mysterious, being under the stars, the galaxies and nebulas, the crisp sky the window to the universe the infinite being and what is that a constellation of? *Well, it kind of looks like an ovary, two eyes and a nose.* Yes, in a peculiar manner of formation. But what came first, the woman or the constellation? Better leave it up for the moon to decipher the stars. But the moon rose ninety degrees west last night; both came first, and before both was the girl, the egg. Finally it made sense. The breath of the land was pulled into the wind. The elements in the setting overpowered the forces of nature, and the next day the sun rose to stillness throughout the valley, birds flying above, blue sky about.

When I went back to San Diego, I took a shower and drank a glass of lemon water at the condo before Kyle picked me up. He had all followed me back to Pacific Beach with Matt and his girlfriend, and by then Kelsey was in Orange County. He drove us across the bay to Ocean Beach. I had not seen Point Loma before, and it seemed like an exquisite prominence of land with a rugged coastline set before the sea on which a bright beach town and other developments were settled. And it seemed similar to Pacific Beach in a way, but it was not until a little later and of a sunset afternoon that I learned of its distinction from all the other neighborhoods in San Diego, and every other neighborhood from each other.

Matt insisted on going to the safari, but before the safari, he wanted to get some cannabis. Our energy had been drained a bit from our stay at the ranch, with the howling winds of the night we stayed up for most of the night both nights. Had we gone to the safari on that day instead of the next, I might have been tired and not as focused or even almost indifferent to all the animals. But they were interesting, mammals and Aves lounging and perched in their respective habitats, some sort of tropical and others more arid but all distinct. I wondered if they play at night after hours. I was not because I was outside, or not outside. Inside, and at the same time, outside. Those animals are wild, and in the wild they must evolve alongside the innovations of man and the environmental impacts. The plains, the jungles, forests, deserts, rivers, deltas, basins are their habitats and even their playgrounds; even the sky, seeing a flock of birds flying by, playing in the air. So, they might have been a bit confused. Then inside they may paw each other almost lasciviously. Graceful, but they take on a different kind of grace, graciousness, taste. There were Covid-19 masks laying around. The tiger sat calm, perched on a wooded surface in a prominent position. The animal thinks, you used to pet me, then suddenly, everyone began wearing face masks. The masks! Those are littered like napkins. I must lay inside, and outside. The okapi just telepathized me, but not me outside, the tiger inside, and he'd like the prize he was promised. As though that's how it started. And then we began the tour.

We saw all the exhibits. We went to a cafe. Kyle and I both ordered a beer. There were two kinds, orange and brown, and that was based on the color of their labels. They were served in a bottle. Mine had a green and bright flavor. Matt and his girlfriend didn't mind waiting for us to finish our orange beer. They were being giddy together, possibly still tired from the ranch. I've experienced from writing when tired—or distressed and in pain from the gut's connection to the brain—creativity can manifest itself suddenly and unusually. Writing into the night as that occurs can be when some wild or winding streams take form. Inspiration lights the pathway in sync with each step. And it was well into the night and deep in the mind when some of the widest streams took course. I rested my mind. At those times, it revolved at full tilt. We finished and walked out to the car. I went back to the condo and dozed off early that night. I had gone out on the balcony for a little while. I dreamt lightly by the moon, and then I woke up to the morning light streaming into my room.

I had just written and put together my first book and completed my undergraduate degree. The joy from finishing that project exceeded any other before then, and I wished to get the book acquired by publishers. It was my first one. With each draft its outline became more distinct and easier to follow. Some of that drive went into applications. But there was Covid-19, and the economy was sort of in a transformative stage at that time, even in limbo. It had to transition to almost exclusively online. I started working for the fleet. I ought to have been writing.

There was an app for the fleet. My work ethic and long hours came from the exertions in literature. It was for a couple of months in San Diego, about the duration of going through the first book for the ultimate time then. There was otherwise not a lot going on then, with Covid-19 happening. Nick posted up inside. He was in graduate studies working on a doctorate degree. He worked for the government but had been taking time off. We usually ran into each other in the morning, mostly when I was in the kitchen making breakfast, before going out. Nick hung out in the condo. Part of his studies may have included listening to podcasts, reading the news, articles, essays, research, watching lectures. With emphasis on facts and statistics, the realm must be three dimensional. One greater may not incorporate either axis in its depth at discourse. It must be a different world, and it may have everything that the conglomeration thinks, everything that the higher realm constitutes. There is only a fourth in the metaphysical sense, so far as abstract theory may be concerned. One that its branches sprouted from, a notion founded upon, a world on the brink of expansion, one of one within a larger world, and one made up of many worlds, like a set of nesting dolls.

Nick was born in Costa Rica and then moved to Pacific Beach in childhood, to the condo. The summer nights are nice. I imagined on the balcony or out on a run the sensation of a dream that must have instilled before and during adolescence. I saw surfing as part of that, something that I had replaced with skateboarding in the summer, and baseball.

At the condo it was Nick, his son, and a third bedroom which they rented out. His area of study was within a field of science, a behavioral or social science. It must have incorporated multiple areas within the broader domain. It may have been supposed at some point of interest that the environment shapes an individual completely, and perhaps that has even influenced genealogy. From a biological standpoint, socialism impacts everything. There are cultures and technologies, fashions and influences, media and motive, or profit. Genealogy might shape an individual literally, but not completely. One's makeup, to an extent, is genetic. One's intelligence, to a lesser extent, may be acquired through genes but formed through one's consciousness, which must be a separate branch of science, distinct from biology, physics, chemistry, perhaps a matter of philosophy. Personality may not be developed through genetics completely, or any other branch of science. One's microbiota is the same: there are environmental, social and dietary factors that contribute to its development. Some faculties are inherent from birth, one being the composition of microbiota, possibly influencing all the above to a great extent. At the time I was on the cusp of figuring out my composition of microbiota, and the problems stemming from that within the body, possibly influenced by a domain greater than the natural world, the science of biology, sociology, the environment—perhaps the universe.

Nick's cousin Leo who was also the landlord slept on the couch downstairs one night. Together they had a joint ownership of the condo. Its design must have been influenced by the climate, the sun, its proximity to the sea, a sense of tranquility. In the morning, I made breakfast, eggs and bacon with corn tortillas. I thought that Leo was another roommate or tenant or simply a visitor at first. He had arrived the night before while I was on the fleet, and when I got home and the lights were off in the living room area, I walked right past him on the couch. He had flown in from Costa Rica that evening. I thought of the forests there, the flora of jungles by the beach so dense under the far-reaching canopies of trees, the light of the sun absorbed before reaching the forest floor from which the sun and open sky behind the trees may not have been seen since the previous time in tranquility. The sky is almost always clear and open, set like a placid lake with crystal water, and one can almost always count on that.

"There are indigenous people. I was down there, I'm from Costa Rica, and I might start a company there. Some of them have to travel a long way for supplies, everything pretty much. It should be easier for them. But delivering it all to them helps, and it creates opportunity."

"That's a good idea. I've kind of been doing that too."

"Right on. Nick said you're always out and about. Salute to you, my brother."

"There have been more challenges and difficulties because of Covid-19."

"Nick said you're enjoying San Diego."

"Yes, a lot. I saw the sunset at sunset cliffs the other day. It was brilliant. I want to try marketing my book a little."

"That's right, you're a writer."

"I like writing. I just wrote my first book."

"Congratulations, that must be exciting."

"Yes, thanks. I worked very hard on it."

"Go on and finish your breakfast."

"It was nice to meet you."

"Have a good day, brother."

Then I went outside and got on the road and joined the Fleet. I had arrived in San Diego with a car in mint condition, and when I went to Los Angeles, the elements had left my car slightly blemished under the front bumper. The roads in some parts were a bit rough. Some felt almost like driving on rocks going over the cracks in the pavement. I had to replace the brake pads after a month, but they had been worn down by the previous owner. Kyle replaced them with a set of new ones. He said that driving on the bumpy roads wears out the vehicle's suspension system. I imagined that, absorbing the forces acting on a vehicle going over uneven pavement. I asked him about the front bumper, the outer shell directly underneath the front bumper that had been scraped. Some parts of the city were seemingly built on coastal canyons. Pulling into a parking lot, or an entrance, a paved way sloping uphill, the front bumper scrapes against the pavement if not at an angle. There was no need to fix the front bumper, he told me, but I did anyway. I had an average car in the area. There were many nice cars, and they all must have turned into a slopped driveway or entrance at some point, going in headlong, at the wrong angle, and scrapped the underside a bit. I saw someone the other day, I told Kirk, pull into the parking lot driving an Audi R8. Got out, and he was wearing jeans and a jacket, that's style. That may have been second to beauty, body, and fashion. I saw all of that on the fleet and off, the beauty of the setting too, the landscape and skyline and sometimes the backdrop of the sea and the sky blending together, accentuating it all. So, at times, it was interesting on the fleet. One could go out for the day, take a break, or call it a day at one's convenience. If someone brings White Claws to a bachelorette party, and if she invites them inside, they can complete the trip and go inside. If the one with ribbons gives them a good tip, they receive all of it. And it must have been a lovely night. The next day, perhaps takes a break. It's at Kate Sessions Park, not the base of Mt. Soledad, like the note from the wife says. No need to sweat it, the air is often cooler atop the mountain. There must be many a misdirection. I went down the south-facing side of the mountain and then stopped at the condo. I changed into a bathing suit and rode one of the bikes to the beach. The blue sky lay overhead. A warm breeze blew in from the west, the sea. And the beach was not that crowded for the weekend. I lay on the sand from midday into the afternoon as the sun cast out over the water and out toward the horizon.

 Drift off into reflection on that section of sand, as the sun reflects off the water in a straight line back to oneself, so I too reflected in the sun. The condo was several blocks from the ocean, about a mile away or a little less. I walked that distance from a sporting goods store once, after buying a pair of dumbbells and carrying them back. They felt increasingly heavier in each arm after every block. The sun was strong but the air was light. I exercised in the morning and added some lifts into the routine, clearing the mind, starting the day refreshed. On the road I thought creatively, abstractly, or I thought about nothing at all. I sometimes took notes on each stop, or break, or else afterward on the balcony. My mind either felt stimulated on the balcony under the stars and the light of the moon with the mild, light air in breeze, or almost like the sky, vast and clear, speckled with light. Only sometimes my perception of mind seemed a bit clouded at that time. I was figuring out my digestive system. After going on a run, both mind and body seemed lighter, clearer, more fluid. I usually went to bed before midnight and woke up before seven in the morning. And there were many mornings waking up to the sound of metal on pavement, a perpetual cling after ding, and practically right next door. A CrossFit gym was located right across the alleyway. The noise of all the activity was mistaken at first for an auto body shop, even though those tend to have more electric, buzzier sounds. I thought that if the gym was arousing me in the morning before having coffee, I want to join them and exercise more routinely and ambitiously. I had signed up earlier and that afternoon one of the instructors called me to consult. She wondered how I had signed up for the gym online. Because of Covid-19, the gym was not supposed to be taking in new members, but she made an exception. She asked if I was in shape, and I said yes I am. And I was. Perfect, and then I was scheduled to go to class at eight in the morning. I was prepared to perform well and exercise adequately, nice, bright and early.

Many nights I went for my usual run around Crown Point, and it always felt refreshing after expending energy in a brisk, fluid manner. A breeze rolls by and cools the body's sweat, going at a consistent, brisk pace. After going on the fleet in the morning, throughout the day, and at night, it was time for a run, I thought, as I pulled into the garage. I opened the door and at the gate out front was a group of people with some drinks. They were looking for a party at eighteen… That's next door, I told them, and then I showed them. The friend who they were surprising was not home. One of the girls opened the gate and at that point I was on the walkway and heading into the condo, going to change and go on my run, then she opened the gate, and the others went in. They offered me one of their seltzers from across the yard. I went over and had one. We sat at the table in the front yard and waited for their friend, who lived at the house and had said to go inside. It was unusual waiting at the table in the front yard, being right next door to the condo and the front yard in which I lived and had worked out earlier that day, separated by some fencing and plants. They asked if they could party in the condo, and I said no. Nick was up, maybe watching tv downstairs. I liked the local programs. Their friend was arriving soon anyway, one of the girls said. Then he arrived and we went inside. Some of them set up a table and played flip cup. Someone else did backflips standing up. Annah and I were sat outside at the table after the others went back inside.

"Was it unexpected meeting us at the gate?" she asked.

"Kind of, but I was intrigued."

A group of girls had been waiting at the gate right as I got back to the condo and was going to go for a run. They put on some music inside. The night went on later than expected, playing games, even dancing. Then in the morning, I made it to the CrossFit class on time and performed well.

The steam from the shower set off the fire alarm. I had heard that can happen, maybe if the steam is dense enough. Then suddenly it stopped, the air thinned, the steam dissipated, and I washed up and dried off. Stagnating particles filled the air in the apartment in Hollywood. Air circulation was minimal. Dust particles may have been absorbed into the water molecules of the steam. The apartment was far different than the condo. I had gone to Los Angeles for a couple days after a month in San Diego. I stayed in Hollywood at night and tried querying my first book to literary agents that day and the next. Annah lived in Santa Monica. I thought about texting her and seeing her again. Annah had an interesting accent, and I thought that her name is too. The way it's spelled set her apart from all the Annas, though pronounced the same, it's a mix between Anna and Hannah, and when I think of Hannah, at one point I felt butterflies or excited. Annah was from Oahu, the island on which her accent must have developed. I reached out to someone in Maui, and his documentary had touched me profoundly, in a way that a novel or book might inspire and someone. I wondered if Maui is the youngest piece of land above the sea on the planet. I asked Annah, and then if she likes coffee. She flipped her hair, yes! I saw her world expanding and her reach too. I tried querying some agents in the literary industry with my first book, trying to expand its world and its reach in a way. I sought representation from an agent because that's generally the first step to getting into the industry. They might be able to land a book deal, and a good one for the next book.

 I dropped off a few copies, from downtown to Santa Monica, with a few stops in between. One literary agent seemed intrigued, and I received an email from her the following day. She wanted me to send her a synopsis for my book and a query letter. She had read the book and thought that it was quite a story. Indeed, I had endured a lot from that ordeal. Her assistant was going to look over the PDF version, and I thought that I was going to work with a literary agent, then publishers. It does not necessarily have the story arc of a movie, and a book does not need one or even a story, but they may have been expecting one that does have the story arc of a movie. The process of writing that book, from trauma and brain injury to essentially learning to write again and then writing a book, each draft, one section, one chapter, one page or paragraph at a time, that all had an arc. If tangible, that arc might have been like the arch in the canyon, one formed naturally, perhaps by God. Light shed through the arc, and some serious parts glistened. It was all under the surface, not the distress, as profound as that was, but the energy to channel all that into creating a book. She said, Andrew, this should be just the start of your writing journey. There are already too many stories like this. I breathed deep. Though heavy in the moment throughout the year of that ordeal about which I wrote, likewise while writing the book, I thought that it's novel. That arc and the path of consciousness too. I thought of the movement of that period, reaching out beforehand, then being messed with and getting the short end of the stick while writing it: quite novel.

And the movement was still happening, along with Covid-19, which was escalating at that time. That movement was global, active in magnitude even in San Diego. It appeared to be on treadmill, with crowds clogging the streets, spray-painting signs, vandalizing, et cetera. I was beyond frustrated, and that was happening almost immediately following the rejection from the literary agent, and she was promoting a book written by others lightly based on all that. It was in Mission Valley I heard that there was immense vandalizing and looting. During the main riots before then, there must have been a lot more, and that occurred seemingly everywhere, even right as I was writing the book, just about finishing that endeavor, and graduating from university. The whole city was jammed, and I was stuck in the middle of it on the fleet. The whole sense of a dream, that dream that one has, working hard at an endeavor and its completion, sank like a turtle into its shell under the distress from all angles, internal and external.

It was a period when there was a pandemic and the whole world seemed chaotic. But what came first, that movement or Covid-19, is almost as philosophical as the chicken and the egg. It was seemingly simultaneous, philosophically a manifestation of consciousness. And I dreamt of having a peace of mind, having a piece of the pie.

I think, understanding the world, seeing it differently, and therefore energy transfers. The way to understand the world may be in a way au naturel, composed of higher energies and consciousness micro and macroscopic. That power may view one as the self they were at the beginning of it all, in development and of developing aspirations and dreams. Mine may have been experiencing that higher energy or power, like discovering some kind of treasure or ore. In the nature of being, those are both external and internal, in essence, inner and outer. What were they like, and what did they like? I remember going about as a young child, outdoors, indoors, and being fascinated by nature, clouds, creation, art, structures, landscapes, cityscapes, even inanimate objects. My mother's hair straightener: the smell of the irons intrigued me, floral, and sort of musky. And the structure of rocks, the shape and texture, and likewise shells. If they were going out, perhaps to the lake, the ocean, a mountain, a restaurant or store, I often tagged along with them and learned about the natural world. About the nature of being, of consciousness. The way, and the way that energy can understand other beings, entities, other forms of consciousness. In a way a software program can understand the programmer, and vice versa.

Despite the frustrations of the fleet, the landscape merged with the cityscape in a relaxed manner, often glowing, shining under the sun.

When I was born, and for a moment as a young child, I did not understand location, the beauty of the setting, until the moment passed and transitioned into memory, the kind that may inspire, like a point in the sky. Having lived in Portland beforehand, the aesthetic of the setting seemed similar in the summer, but along the way the transitions varied, largely shaped by the landscape, the climate, or the change of climate, the blend of aesthetic. I lived on the peninsula for a couple years, a period in which I wrote my first book, and in a couple of months I might have experienced more of San Diego than

I did of Portland in that time. I might have felt more attached to San Diego than to Portland, or perhaps to any other place in the country, except for maybe the vast world of Los Angeles and the whole metropolis about me, from the walks, the hikes, meditations in the afternoon, and from creating this world of abstraction. I have created this world from inspiration, from the idea of innatism, the profound depths of consciousness stretched by contusion the live memory within and I have built again; one builds memory and then intelligence and likewise builds upon consciousness.

I saw close to every neighborhood in San Diego. On the cliffs of Point Loma I stood and faced the expansive Pacific, wondering of what is shaped by nature what more can be vivid and masterfully blended than such a setting? Foam frothed to the brim of the rugged landscape from which serene seascapes are faced with great pleasure. Down below an octopus twists and twirls in the incoming swell like a pig's tail. The sun is golden, and now orange, and now red, and at last, below the horizon. Behind palm trees, behind Sunset Cliffs, sits a slight incline on which abodes poke up to prominence up and over hilltop, down to the chain restaurants, stores and shops of the Midway District, the first stop off the Five, the loop around the Point, along Rosecrans Street to Nimitz Boulevard, one takes a shortcut to the sunset. I saw a sailboat and set sail across Mission Bay, and at the sight of Sea World I think of the whales playing in the water, and whales in the sea surfacing for a quick body brush, a spout and squee. The octopus dances, with the whale's message in a bottle, written in its ink: I love you. The sailboat sails on. I land on Mission Beach and go along the boulevard and to the left is Belmont Park. In both directions toward the ocean and toward the bay are many side streets and a sense of intimacy. At day and under the moonlight waves break light in flow. I think of yoga on the beach, and then I'm in Pacific Beach. I had thought of Pacific Beach as my childhood beach, the widths of each similar. I went to Los Dos for breakfast and ordered extra green sauce. A bit further north is Bird Rock and then La Jolla, one point to the other on the island of Coronado. Third Street, Fourth Street, out to the beach. The only toll booth collected no toll, and there is a party on the beach, bordered by sea plants sprawled on the sand. The tide had been out and then starts to come in. I cross the bridge to downtown and

Island Ave to Petco Park, and at last, the Gaslamp Quarter. The climate is pleasant, going up the street to Little Italy, pleasing the bustle the whole aesthetic featuring the summer sunset. A vivid view of the sky changing hue going through Golden Hill opens up. I cut through Balboa Park and go to North Park, then down to South Park. Along Fern Street, both sides are lightly lined with flowering trees, Jacarandas. All around are quaint restaurants, and all around every neighborhood is delicious food, everything from pho to foie gras. I ate at a local deli and market, four street tacos, dos asadsa y dos asado, fresh from the kitchen, grilled chicken and steak. Without onions, those might not be high in fodmaps, but if they were, they were delicious before realizing the need to follow the low-fodmap diet.

In Portland, I lived on the peninsula and got to know downtown like much of San Diego. Walking on the street, sidewalks, pathways during the day, afternoon and at night, I learned the area altogether as a conglomeration of continuous urban space. The architecture, engineering, culture, art, shops, halls, venues, food and drink and more made up as much of the setting as the geography of the area did, the bay in which settlers first sailed, and the land on which the city was first developed. There was charm, in the springtime with the fresh blooms and fall with the autumn foliage. The habitants of the city in part make up its culture, the fishing industry, the fresh seafood, the creativity. An accent may be developed, but I had no accent and wrote with no accent. My building manager was from Santa Monica, and she had a mix of both accents. She came into the loft to change a lightbulb one time, and she thought that I had set up the apartment well. I wrote my first book in it. There was not as prominent or pronounced of an accent in San Diego, but sometimes subtle, pacific, and relaxed. There must have been at least a dozen neighborhoods or localities with several more within each, and altogether each one had its own distinctive culture. They are all almost like distinct towns and cities within a greater metropolis. Recognizing neighborhoods and the transitions between one and the other was easy, usually with some kind of separation between each setting, whether a body of water, a freeway, a geographic feature, or urban development marked the partitions. Maybe one of the best neighborhoods is Pacific Beach. For some, it might be by a park or on a canyon or near the ocean or further inland. I was near the ocean and all throughout had style and class, the cars, boats, landscapes, designs, and dress. Sandals were popular. The most comfortable footwear might be the sandal, and the easiest to slip on, more so than the slipper. In a Mediterranean, kind of tropical climate, the sandal can be worn inside and outside. I wore sandals everywhere in San Diego, at the beach, to the store, on a bike, out to eat, but not on a run, or at a class. I laid down in bed one night with my sandals on, and even though they fell off my feet overnight, I slipped into them in the morning ready for breakfast.

Some restaurants, and one I frequented often, offered me juice drinks upon my arrival. One time, I was at a restaurant and there was someone waiting and the hostess said that both of our orders will not be ready for up to thirty minutes. We were offered juice drinks, and after having those, slightly sweet, hibiscus-flavored tea drinks, we both went across the street for a beer and tacos. It was Jean Paul, and he was from Germany. He almost didn't seem old enough to legally drink alcohol, but he could drink a beer fast.

"How many gulps will I take to drink this pint of beer?" he asked. "Only two."

He demonstrated, and he was right. He was right every time. Just like a funnel. Yet no matter how much beer he drank and food he ate he said that he stayed skinny. I pictured him during Oktoberfest, and all the others carousing about the venues and streets. It must have been wild. Dear John, you're a different kind of human being. I'm a simple person but sometimes think differently. That can be abstract, ordinary and extraordinary. Isn't that consciousness, connecting tenses, past, present, and perspective with abstract thought? Solving a Rubik's Cube blindfolded may even stimulate it, the esoteric phenomenon.

Jean Paul raised his glass, gulped it down, then placed it dry on the table.

I went to Balboa Park to go for a walk, and I watched some people playing tennis for a moment from the pathway. Two gentlemen practiced on the court. I only watched half a set, and then I made my way to the heart of Balboa Park. The botanical garden was closed because of Covid-19, and the museum around the corner was too. Walking about were many families, individuals, groups, and possibly tourists, some wearing face masks and others not. Branches blew in the breeze and leaves glistened in the sun. I followed a path straight to the Japanese garden and went in, musing on tranquility, digressing into the still of the moment. The calmness of water gently flowing over rocks, pearling in the air, cascading, balancing the moment continued in uniform motion. The leaves to the breeze their own trickle. Standing on the front veranda of the Minka structure, elevated a few feet above the pond, typified the Japanese garden. Koi fish swam below in shoals, and the most transcendent of the pack decorated in a pattern of vibrant colors led the others in unison, wafting through the water around the oasis, occasionally twirling under the waterfall.

A large group of tourists approached the pond and the house from the path above. The one in front took pictures of the landscape, the pond, the decorated coy fish. "It's Him!" Perhaps it is, through a kind of omnipresence, but in a calm, somewhat ornate form. I went and checked out the store behind the structure.

Later that day I was on the fleet, or the next day, or the next. Suddenly it became almost like a maze, a labyrinth, a Rubik's Cube with four dimensions. I went for a run one night and meditated down to the bay, by the salty tree, reflecting off the water the moonlit streak, its canopy branching into the star-filled sky, then around the point, up the stairs and along the sidewalk and side of the street. I was into writing books, a field trip to prehistoric foundations rooted in consciousness. Like a museum for prized artifacts, often only bits and parts of relics are showcased. It could be an adventure, inner more so than outer, but perhaps both. I run back to the condo and go upstairs and start writing a new book immediately, I thought, but the idea of starting a new book was daunting to me. *A book won't write itself, Andrew!* The more I thought about the Rubik's Cube, the more the idea was making an impression on me, and the more I enjoyed the idea of writing a new book. I thought of getting a writer's den in Los Angeles, and right around the corner there could be a literary publisher, an editor, agent, or manager on their own kind of writing journey through others or within. That night I saw the beach and the bay twice, clear sky and stars, dotting the darkness of an interwoven consciousness. Then I turned the corner and went up to Hornblend and that's when I decided to start a new book, this book.

The previous one turned over like a leaf in the wind, the way it rolls from within, and I soon began it.

In the afternoon I went to a market store and left a box of books outside by the entrance, coming straight from the store after picking it up. I left the box outside instead of bringing several copies of my first book inside and getting groceries. I was quick and thought that the box will be fine outside for a minute—maybe not even one minute, but ten seconds to the refrigerator and thirty at the register. When I went outside, the box was gone. That was Hollywood. I walked up the hill. It took a couple of years, drafts and versions to try and get the book right, first learning to write again, and then learning to write a book. Thinking back to it, the time that it took to create the first three books could be a book in itself, that whole period as a separate journey into the past, and the time of creation as a sequel to the book created. But the thought of thinking about the past in the past is mind-boggling, as though it is its own tense, its own syntax. How to begin is almost puzzling. Starting with creation, at the end of the period being created, and then going backward throughout that period but forward in what is being created is almost like a kind of timelessness. The end of the period as the beginning, or the beginning as the end, transitioning to the subsequent period of creation. At the beginning I had almost no confidence that I could write a book but determination to complete the endeavor. It was difficult to do, following serious injuries, with distress, but without any sort of training. I was creative, and my body and brain were rebounding, but to create through writing? I didn't think that I was born under that kind of star originally, but upon regaining consciousness from comatose, those faculties seemed to suddenly enable. That I had just been walking among the stars right before my box of books was taken rankled me, the rest of the way up the hill, I had but a bag of groceries. Those books took about four months to recompose, and about two years from starting the first draft of the first version to try and make it better, get it right, as well as I was able to then. I went to San Diego as soon as I finished writing and editing it, as well as the two preceding versions. Altogether it took three compositions, several drafts, and a busy period of exertion and focus to complete that painstaking project. I often thought of the period about which I was writing, going through it all, sort of reliving it in memory. It had the combined effect of everything in that period as one feeling, joining the joys and pains. I tread in the present for a break from that focus only occasionally, in a different light, with a different perspective, either stimulated or spent and often satisfied with the progress. As it was all experienced almost anew, the idea of consciousness changed form and expanded. I dedicated a lot of energy to writing the book, to figuring out how to write the book, through its completion. I was a student at that time, completing a bachelor's degree, which made the endeavor a bit more demanding, sometimes digressing from the middle of one stream of consciousness to a completely different realm, on a different medium, and part of a curriculum. It may have been for a moment, an hour, a day, afternoon and evening, and then that stream of consciousness resumed slightly askew to the stream that was developing at the time of digression. Even sometimes in class I was thought about working on my book. During Covid-19, classes were online, and the transition from that project to another or to other material was smooth. Because of Covid-19, I wanted to rework or actually completely rewrite my first book, from the first two versions of the book. During that period, that movement developed and took off all around the world and right outside, as I was beginning to be exploited. I stayed inside, worked on my book and finished my undergraduate degree, hoping that it surpasses the inspiration of the first two versions.

There were face masks to wear, as per ordinances, but I seldom wore one. In San Diego, biking around the point or on Mission Boulevard, at the central park or on the cliffs at sunset, not many people wore a facemask either. Since the beginning of Covid-19, and after five months of ordinances and regulations, everyone must have been eager for medical advancements and remission in numbers, to lift the codes and recover the energy, the economy, the bustle as before. Everywhere daily operations changed and suddenly many switched to operating online, affecting the inner workings and mechanisms of consciousness, maybe largely changing cognition, even physiology. To write a book amid that happening may have synergized all three. The universe had opened up, in a way, around the time when I decided to rework the book and begin to draft. After all, the first two versions of it had been composed under distress, that feeling from the ordeal, sort of overpowering at times, influencing the way the craft developed and the stream for that period emerged. To write one must sit down or stand up and write. That may be the starting point to experiencing magic. An artist, using heart, spirit and energy to synergize creativity, may recreate a notion of consciousness as such.

It was during that period when the creator within began to emerge. A good run interspersed developed that faculty, and so did an interest in medicine. The drive to create endured, maintaining a high output and fast pace throughout.

For my first book, I established that pace. The whole world sort of paused momentarily and then what finally emerged was a book from the energy within, using heart, spirit and mind. For that period of creation, a lot of energy was exerted. I sometimes heard Phil, and this was in Portland, whine about something and then finish the rant with "Man!" I had heard it when I first started the project. In a way, he was an artist, because he played the guitar, and he had a big gut. On the contrary, I began to get even leaner—and that was before figuring out my digestive system and rebalancing my microbiome, a period after passing kidney stones the first time, when my abdomen and its inner workings seemed to function and felt anew, but only for a moment.

In Portland I ran maybe four times a week. I went from Congress to Spring Street, then cut over to the Western Promenade, and along Danforth to John Ford's statue. Then I ran up the hill to Congress and crossed the street and went down the hill a few hundred feet to the Wadsworth, into the loft, and worked on my book. That burst of exertion created energy. It seemed not only replenished but enhanced. During Covid-19, and my last semester of undergraduate study, I had a routine. I got up, worked out. Ate food, wrote. Sometimes I wrote all day. There was a lot of coursework, but it seemed to be a reduced load in light of the online operations. I was not on a fast, or an intermittent fast, but a diet high in omega-3s. At night, I did schoolwork, and likewise upon waking up in the morning. Before Covid-19, I worked more in that period about which I've written, and the routine was almost overwhelming. Distracted by my consciousness, I wrote more. I ate, worked out, digressed, went in my study, into lucubration, and went to bed.

By working out, it was not only the run around the peninsula, but climbing mountains in the living room afterward too. It was jumping rope outside the bathroom. It was walking out on the wooden plank hands first, pushing down for ten and sitting up for twenty. It was burping the highest burpee. At one point, Tiffany heard some of the workouts, especially the burpees. She lived below me and maybe wondered about the noise with the regulars outside. On the stoop, they smoked, and sometimes she joined them out on the stoop with cannabis. I exercised whenever I had the moments to spare. Ten to eleven at night on average. I ate mindfully, exercised regularly, and during the second set of the workout Tiffany texted me. I had to cut corners in a way and finish the circuit in the morrow. After she came in from the stoop one time a while earlier, I learned that we were neighbors, only vertically. I was twenty-two and she was twenty-five. I stepped out one morning and found a note on my doormat that said she wanted to hangout sometime. I mentioned it to my friend at work, Zach, and he thought that it was an intriguing inquiry. The hardwood maple floors can be loud, the creak and groan, standing while writing. It was expanding the domain of creation in one's element, then going right into the exercises. The building was named after a poet, a writer, and in his namesake building I was also writing, but much more prose than poetry.

Since the day I sent the first manuscript of the first version of the first book to Nas in New York, I sometimes sent letters that I had written with the passion that one has to write a book. They were brief yet kind of long letters, usually after completing a book or manuscript, excited, or else in distress. External and internal factors influenced their composition. Reading them, and their accompanied writing, I will probably see that my writing has improved since then, at the time of writing this. Then and now I can read this writing and loose its tracks in the past, the early expansion of mind, the course of consciousness.

I was trying to get my first book published traditionally and be a prolific writer in the literary industry, and I thought that he might be able to help. Thinking of that exertion of mind in a time of recreation is almost as daunting as it was starting the endeavor, trying to create an intricate composition.

All the writing from that beginning expansion, that course of consciousness, happened at the Wadsworth in my writing spot. The Wadsworth had some unique tenants, and the apartments were original by design, with a brick exterior, ship's wood flooring, tiling, high ceilings. I had been inside Tiffany's apartment, and it was bright red and decorated with art. The inside of mine was painted sky blue. Every floor was painted a different color, red, blue, brown, yellow, green, and turquoise. I thought that the floor on which my apartment was located looked the best. Going down the high hallway painted sky blue was calming, with light fixtures on either side lighting the space, like a quick walk outside under the blue sky and sun. Kara lived on my floor. It was not until later, in the midst of that setting under blue sky and sun, that I let her know that I was wild for her. I ought to have left her a note, like Tiffany had with a bottle of wine. I was into red wine and tannins at that time. I decorated my kitchen with a few bottles of wine, some full, and of some only displaying the corks. I liked my writing spot, as a twenty-year-old, twenty-one, twenty-two, as it were, working on my first book.

The apartment itself was called the Wad. The ceiling opened up further inside to a high space full of light, seeping into the other rooms, the loft, each nook and cranny of my writing spot. On summer days, sunlight streamed into the main room and up along the sky-blue walls, making the whole place suddenly feel open and big. During spring, many indoor plants bloomed and each one grew lush after the winter. With reduced natural light and no direct sunlight shining through the big northwest-facing window, they had been dormant. The sun dipped behind an adjacent building in the afternoon before setting for the night. Then all of a sudden there were longer days and brighter light, or the opposite, shorter days and reduced light, signifying the solstice, the distinct, sometimes sudden seasonal changes. The Wad had some decorations, furniture, appliances, a workspace, but not a lot of open space that can refresh the mind and filter one's energy, like water flowing through rocks. In some of the open space I worked out. I even thought about putting a rowing machine in the Wad and incorporating that into the routine: rowing every day, along with exercising the mind, and sitting on the couch at night with candlelight and expending that filtered energy. A big window and doorway with great wood frames were positioned on either end of the space in which I wrote. At one point, because of its size, the windowsill in the living room became my workspace between desks. There was as much room to work on the sill as there is on a school desk or more, and beside the swiveling chair was a coffee table. I drank plenty of coffee, and on the table was a lot of paper, some folders, pens, and organizers, a decoration and statue.

Looking out the window spanned a view of the landscape behind the neighboring buildings and others sloping down the hill. Late spring comes to mind: in the morning the sunrise and at night the sunset, red and orange, tinting the clear sky and sometimes painting the cloud cover those vibrant colors. The trees had awakened from dormancy and began growing leaves bright green and buds flowering pearl white, pink and magenta. The sun shone and the sky around appeared light blue, lighter than the blue of the room, the clouds soft and plump, floating in the light wind. A big mountain stood off in the distance. Its prominence was only somewhat discernible. The summit coated in snow reflected the sun and the sky's glow. In the evening, that glow stretched over the landscape and the city below, undulating at the horizon, in waves of passion, radiating over the background and view. The glow, it seemed, formed as though out of the blue, the sky, the layer between day and the vast space beyond at night. The streetlights shone on the ground like stars. I recalled thunderstorms and lightning, the church bell ringing, fog rolling in, the sky clearing up. I smelled the tide, food and coffee.

Off to the side of the apartment and hugging the wall was a ladder staircase, connecting the main floor to the lofted space where I had put my bed and decorated the banister with lighting. Someone asked if I had fallen down the ladder, because it was steep and it creaked lightly, like unfinished stairs painted white. I did fall down that ladder staircase once. That happened during an evacuation around the time when Covid-19 started. Philbrook, who had a gut, must have been worked up about something. Amid a dream, the fire alarms went off and through the noise he shouted, "Man!" Someone had left a candle and wax paper in the oven, he mentioned later. I had been in bed, laying down for a moment, and when the fire alarms rang and I got out of bed and hurried to the ladder I experienced a head rush from rising so fast and then fell down the ladder right onto the cushion of a kind of bulbous furniture.

The first few months at the Wad were somewhat of a blur. I commenced the endeavor right away, and writing was difficult at first, following the ordeal and recovery, learning the craft and finding a groove. The motivation came from the recovery. Abdominal pain had been pronounced at times before then. The demand of writing a hundred-page book one page in seemed overwhelming, but I recall the excitement of starting the first draft, mainly because I had been quite distressed after the ordeal. It was a small apartment. I brought the sofa and bed up the flights of stairs, then arranged those and set up the rest of the space. I had placed the furniture precisely, and in an open area at the bottom of the staircase ladder I positioned a cushioned furnishing against the wall. The sofa lay in an alcove under the loft. Soon after starting the book on the coffee table, I went to the bookstore across the square. I met Sara inside. I went in to ask about writing a book and Sara was working behind the counter. We met for coffee later and went over the project that I was beginning to work on. I didn't have the slightest idea of how to write a book, and there was no better place to start that book, the first book, than at the beginning. And the beginning seemingly began after waking up from the coma. I wrote the first five thousand words in the first week. It was the first draft, and that became the outline. Everything thereafter formed the foundation for the book, when everything from the ordeal was fresh in my mind. Some recollections have endured more than amnesia, than timelessness, appearing vivid with even a slight spark in consciousness. Many are heartening, and some are hard to bear. I thought of my abdomen, my digestive system in distress, and working through IBS then.

We met every week, Sara and I, sometimes for coffee or tea. Whether at a cafe or at the bookstore or at my apartment, I had a new chapter or section of the book that she went over as I wrote on. She didn't help with the writing itself, learning to write a book and developing the craft, but she proofread that draft and motivated me to write. She read a book written entirely punctuated with commas. Thinking of styles, in contrast, I must have read books with prose that almost never used commas, and I liked it. The tempo of various styles of prose can flow across the page, and that's how I tried to craft my writing. That may have been the case at first, and then that flow became more natural. Sometimes it came in long spurts, sitting down at the computer, or in short spurts, leading to notes. In the beginning, with Sara, I never slacked off and progressed with the project. The output was consistent, but if one week I had extra then that was all right. The condition in which I wrote that first draft was sultry, and that caused me to perspire lightly while writing, like a mind-body workout. The Wad at that time did not have central air conditioning, and I was too engrossed in the endeavor to get a fan. Then I did, and it was one with a spritzer. I suppose the mist refreshed the mind. It had an invigorating sensation, slipping into a meditative state for a moment, then resuming. I had heard that when the brain is exerting substantial energy it burns more calories than perhaps a body does while running. The energy exerted may be equal to the relative conditioning of the body and the brain. However, though I was an avid runner and writer, the scale stayed the same throughout the entire summer. Finishing the first draft at the end of August allowed for a small period to organize my material before my schedule filled and before I started working on the second draft. It was the jog before the run, stretching out, warming up, and then it was essentially the run itself from the energy exerted. A draft in manuscript form sat on the table beside the desk and acted as motivation to transform that pile of paper into a book. Once I finished the draft, I went hiking on a mountain.

 I took a day trip to the northeastern coast. It was pleasant time of year right before the beginning of autumn. There were some mountains and hills along the rugged coast, some areas of prominence obscured by thin cloud cover, but most of the landscape in view sat under the clear sky. I started the hike on a section of rocks and boulders piled at the base of a mountain and went over and atop the scramble and found a trail. It went alongside the northern face of the mountain and a rock wall that went straight up to the top. The trail sort of zig-zagged up the rock face along which iron rails and rungs had been installed in parts. The expanse opened as the elevation surpassed that of the surrounding geography. Toward the summit, all the land inland stretched to the horizon. It may have been sunny in my spot while the space behind was clouded over. At the top, in every direction lay the ocean. Everything was sort of grey under the cloud cover, even inland. Only where the sky had openings light fell through, and it was golden light, light that might seem to shine brighter at the end of a rain shower.

After that, my writing improved. Or the stream rolled on the page more fluidly, and I was in a grove. I lived in downtown, the Old Port was a quick walk away, and connected to my building was a good local bar. Though I didn't go to the bar often, I liked its decor and interior set up. Every Wednesday was free pinball night and along every wall there was a different machine. Some rooms were full of pinball machines, old-school games, another had videogames, and the main room had tables and maybe board games. Above the bar were TVs that played trivia at night.

I brought my laptop to the bar to try and write. It was snowing outside and seeing it through the window seemed almost magical. Perhaps the day before it was sort of dreary. Sometimes it snowed, and during the snowfall the atmosphere seemed almost magical, then after it snowed it blended with the cityscape stained with sand and salt. The bar had specials during snowstorms. I sat before the wintery scene outside, the snow falling heavily through the air, accumulating on the ground, on cars and objects, slowly rising like bread leavening. I put my laptop into my backpack, paid and went to the Wad. Then I received a phone call.

The phone rang again. It was Katie. "Hey, Katie."

"Hey," she said. "Guess where I am right now?"

"Where?"

"Arcadia. I have tons of work to do. Come down and have a beer with me."

"Someone said the next time you call money bread you will be paid in sourdough, and I know you like spelt."

"What?"

"Right now?"

"Yes!"

"I'm writing right now."

"Same! Well just about to. Come down, I'll buy you a drink."

"I'm going to play pool."
"Play pool?"
"Yeah, billiards."
"Oh, *cool*."

I had seen Katie at the store, and she was there with her friend Eve getting a bite to eat. Katie was fond of Eve, who was completely her own unique individual. She was a witch, I think, a Witch of the Down East, which may have been a kind of sisterhood or organization that practiced mysticism. She read tarot cards and led cartomancy workshops. I went to a class and remember feeling transcendental as Eve walked around the candlelit room with special incense and relaxing music playing softly from the walls. On her desk sat a powerful stone. What its powers were may have been mystical, and it accentuated the ambiance of the setting set in the center of the room. I sat next to the powerful stone and felt as though I was absorbing its energy. Some people took notes, at least one woman. Most of the guests were girls and women, all attuned to the stone. In the candlelight it seemed to emit tangible energy, like smoke from burning incense rising in the air. Hallie was taking notes, and she offered to send them to me after class. A little later I learned that Hallie enjoyed playing billiards. She knew how to play well, and she beat me in a variety of games five times out of ten. My stroke fascinated her because to her I had an unusual one but usually scored. We played a few games each time and the games often varied, but always on a pocket table, and always for fun. Instead of playing pool one night we ate dinner at a Thai restaurant. There was an unexpected snowsquall going on and walking up the hill and down the street to the restaurant was even exciting. And it was down that hill at the end of the night that ended up being slippery, because of the icy conditions, and because I had eaten well I insisted on walking it off. I set off down the street through the snowfall, and then after turning the corner down the hill I stepped on a steel plate and slid along its surface balanced. Firmly planted, I got a nod hello and have a good night.

That snow squall signified the beginning of winter, and I wrote through the holiday season and then the new year and into January. To wind down and finish that draft of the first version of my first book inspired a sense of creation within. Many times I thought of giving up the endeavor, gaining energy and doing it later, but the creator within sought a sense of achievement. I thought of the time on the train when the passenger talked on the phone about a presentation at work, and that was at a university, when someone had inspired the room by giving a presentation on their story. I finished in the middle of January, a full manuscript. Although my writing had improved from the first draft, from learning to write a book and learning the craft, I had rushed to complete throughout the fall, and the brain injury from which I may have still been recovering influenced that writing. It may have been two dimensional, absent of all the other dimensions that may make up consciousness. Regardless, I was thrilled to complete it. I wondered before anyone or anywhere else if I should send the manuscript to Nas, thinking of when I regained consciousness at Mass General and was asked who my favorite rapper was. Then at that moment, a loud horn honked outside. I thought yes. He had inspired me in a way to start writing my first book when I did and to continue working on it to its completion. Later that week or the next I met up with Sara and asked if she could look over the manuscript. Said it was much better than my writing the previous summer. I thought it might be good to try to publish it traditionally in the literary industry, or even through the industry elite. I thought that I could make it with my first book, and that by querying the manuscript to agents and publishers I could achieve that before the book was even published: making it to the Big Five, the publishing houses, or their imprints. Before the ordeal, I read and wrote for leisure on occasion. Then throughout the recovery, I became more of an avid reader, and I read mostly in spurts at first because my mind fogged up from injury, almost like it had been upon regaining consciousness, but not completely. Soon after all the injuries healed, the fog began to clear up, and then distress shone through and was perceived in each dimension. Once recovered and cleared for exercise, some of that distress and restlessness assuaged, and light trickled in. All the while I had been reading in spurts, gradually increasing those to longer durations, and the fog gradually eased on its own up until right about when I started the endeavor of writing a book.

    That first draft was difficult to complete. The lingering effects of TBI dissipated after completing it and celebrating through hiking, and those had been diminishing from all the reading and writing. I was working at a library behind the desk, finishing my undergraduate degree, and I thought that maybe by being around so many books, it might be easier to traditionally publish mine. It seemed like it could have fallen into place. A group of literary agents came to the library, accepting queries. But after querying my first book, once the manuscript was refined and formatted into a book, I was rejected and then decided to publish it myself.

During the winter and into the summer I continued working at the library, and in the middle of spring I finished working on my first book. The head librarian, Lora, was spiritual. I mentioned that I was dating a spiritual girl, and Lora said that she must be a strong woman. She is, I thought. In tune with her own spirituality, and conscious of some kind of higher energy. And perhaps consciousness is the energy, expanding the universe to try and create more conscious activity. Every now and then she might have gone to a potluck dinner, once in a blue moon, and I thought that when the moon is full, she might get together with the witch sisterhood, and Lora could have been one of the sisters. Lora had been at the library for a while, and she was familiar with its systems, operations, order, and organization. I remembered walking through the doors and looking at the main display case of books and having the ambition of getting mine on there, of it being everywhere, and then sitting down and working on it after completing the duties. Every hour I had to survey each floor from the seventh floor down and count and record the number of patrons on each floor. At the front desk on the first floor, other librarians worked on something else or relaxed, provided guidance or direction, as I completed the daily tasks. The sixth floor had the best view, and I remember seeing the Wad across the way, the cherry blossoms out front, the cobalt water of the bay, shining in the sun. Later I came across some international students jumping barefooted over a set of fully enclosed display tables on the fourth floor, and inside housed some artifacts from a period in history and off to the side sat the girls eating hamburgers, and I remember being surprised by it all. Down on the first floor the other librarians were astonished. Also on the fourth floor, a patron, Tim, sometimes drank in the lounge area. He was a burly man with long grey hair down to his chest, and he was not the only one to utilize the fourth floor in a similar way, that is to say, like the studious patrons. Someone who was there with Tim one time said that he was trying to keep his spot on the fourth floor all to himself. That was good, because the fourth floor could sometimes get out of hand. One time a woman was there with him, and they kissed passionately on the couch. Not just the couch, everywhere on the fourth floor, in fact. Then it may have been the following week when Tim drank too much wine and passed out in the corner. The paramedics had to lift him up onto a stretcher, and because he was quite big, it turned out to be a bit difficult. A couple of patrons on the fourth floor assisted, and then when Tim was lifted onto the stretcher, he let out a belch. Lora had known him for a while. "Tim's really good," she said. "Back in the day he conjured ghosts. He had all the equipment." I thought of Ghostbuster equipment, cameras and suits. She laughed. "Hey, remind me to tell Ally the next time I see her, she can't let her friends all horse around on the fourth floor again!"

I was perplexed, and then at the Wad I got back into my element. The apartment was maintained well, and it was somewhat neat and organized. I had my primary laptop and another one that I used like a typewriter, only to write. There were some books, textbooks, notebooks, folders, paper and papers. I exercised inside, before a run or after, but that's more of an energy than an element. There was a gym nearly connected to the building one or two doors down the block and on occasion I attended an afternoon class. It was around that time during finals when exhaustion kicked in and I got the flu. I had finally finished my first book and published it a week earlier, after working on it deep into the night every day since starting the manuscript. The goal was to not only write but create a book before I had planned to graduate from college had I not endured that ordeal. I did that with a week to spare, two years after the ordeal, starting the endeavor right after fully recovering from it. I had endured a lot of distress before and as I was writing, but following its completion, I felt somewhat pleased.

Then there was the class on Wednesday at the gym, after regaining some energy, conditioning the mind—all the quick sets, always in motion, a fast-paced exercise. Dizzily, I walked off to the bathroom and sipped some water from the fountain and then resumed the circuit, keeping in mind a flow, an effortless distribution of energy, as though running. Toward the end of class a few women were peeking my way, maybe because I was the youngest in class, and it was a hard class. I rowed on the machine between circuits. The whole motion of rowing is a seemingly effortless production of energy, like the exterior of a turbine. I finished the final circuit for class with some energy left over and then headed to the locker room.

That night started sort of romantically on a pier. The water as a mirror of beauty reflected the energy in the universe. In the morning, I almost aced the final exam. I had done well on the other four also. I went to the apartment afterward and lay back for a moment on the couch, contrary to the upright posture on the writing machine.

Around that time the number of patrons in the library started to go down for the summer vacation. The count dropped on each floor except the fourth floor and a few more characters arrived at the beginning of summer. Patrons of the library mostly used it for reading. Zach and I managed the library at night in the summer. It was just us at the circulation desk, and the nightly duties were reduced only to the head count every hour and being attentive. We tried doing creative collaboration, and occasionally for me, taking notes. At that point, I still felt some of the thrill from completing that first book, but that had started to wane. To try and secure a book deal in the literary industry, I went to New York seeking literary agents and publishers.

Sometimes Zach put songs together at his apartment and at the library. He sang and made his own instrumentals electronically, combing both to produce songs. He didn't play instruments but wanted to learn to play the guitar, and I did too. Zach suggested we record some songs, and he then explained the technique, pitches, bars, snares, kicks, loops, and timing, tempo. After all the writing then, learning and focusing on the craft, Zach was impressed. I had suggested writing to him, creating a book, novel, novella, even short stories. And he had written. There may be no greater endeavor than creation, and it can produce an even greater feeling of excitement upon completion. He had commenced a book at his apartment but writing one was more than he had thought it might be. After that, we were back on the track and put together a few songs. I was striving for four; before New York I only finished two. We recorded two songs, I suppose, in two days. I had gotten ahead of myself. I was trying to impress Nas. Maybe it was, for that endeavor following the ordeal, injuries, seizures, and fog. I wrote it when I was 21 and

22. I had just made a couple of songs and was going to New York, trying to make it, an opportunity in the literary industry, from all the expansive energy that went into creation.

I am in the Lower East Side. I had walked from 42nd Street down 1st Avenue after riding in a bus all morning. Along 1st Ave, I felt some sweat on my chest. I had stepped off the bus in a rush, it was already early afternoon and there was no time to waste. I had walked and I had perspired, I had stopped at a Halal cart for a napkin, but napkins were for customers, the proprietor said. Just one to dab the sweat, beading a bit in the sun. A local at the cart recommended the coffee shop around the corner, and then showed me and made sure I had plenty of napkins. Wait, how about a damp cloth. I placed it on the nape of my neck and cooled off.

All throughout that weekend, it seemed like everyone was down to earth. It was hot in New York. I thought about all the walking in the humidity. Among all the mighty skyward structures, I did not see the big apple. I saw a maze of masonry.

I continued down 1st Avenue and the heat and moisture rose from the ground up it seemed. I thought that I was sweating, perspiring under my arms, and from my chest. After a couple miles and after passing more carts I finally made it to a baggage storage, a small convenience store, where I held my suitcase and backpack through the afternoon. I got the envelope for Nas from its spot on top neat, with a letter inside and a couple of songs produced at the library. I also brought a copy of the book, and I was going to reach out to literary agents and publishers after that and the next day.

I went out and the sun shone down even stronger. By the time that I made it to Broadway I was almost sweating again. Then, just as I passed between pedestrians on the sidewalk, an Amazon representative came up to me. There were a few, and they were standing in front of the big entrance. They were all trying to usher us inside. "Come inside," one representative said to me. "Check it out. It's free!"

"Yes?"

"It's the grand opening, it's a party!"

"Okay."

I opened the tinted door and a cool draft of air rushed past me pulled from outside. It was dark inside, some spaces under blacklight, and on each wall were digital projections of Amazon products. I walked through a room and moving along the floor, walls, and ceiling in a perpetual wavelike rhythm were the cover images of hundreds of Amazon Original movies and shows. They were all moving rapidly in every direction, some expanding in size and along with them Amazon was also expanding. The whole display of shows must have been orchestrated by an intelligent being, and it was as though the images, the room and I were all moving in one fluid motion. In almost no time vertigo took effect and all around me I heard distorted sound effects and my own voice. Isn't this cool, Oceane? Hey, it's your show! A man asked where's the bathroom? I pointed toward the basement which had a restroom sign hung above the doorway. Oceane went that way. I decided to check it out, to wash my face and freshen up, and even the bathroom was illuminated under blacklight. The mirror seemed opaque, and my reflection appeared like the moon in the sky on a foggy night. Then I went back upstairs and then outside and down the street on Broadway to his company office. I pressed the buzzer and then inside the lobby waited for a minute. I thought about Nas being up in the office. I had no speech but ambitioned a deal in the literary industry. I climbed the stairs and went in.

Nas was not in the office workspace. I left the envelope and book for him with the woman behind the desk. She lightly flipped through the pages and picked up the envelope and said that they'll be given to him. With that, I thanked her and drank a glass of lemon water and then went outside.

I started going north along Broadway. I wished to say, I've gotten a bit better at writing since that manuscript, as the sun shone down on her from over the sea.

I walked ahead in the afternoon heat and then someone conducting a survey pulled me aside for a moment. Who did I think is the best president in United States history? George Washington, I said. There is a mountain named after him, and he fathered the country. How old am I? I was twenty-two then, and I had just been in over my head with passion. She hadn't thought of it that way. That was part of creation. With that, she was taken aback. Thought that I was nineteen, because she was nineteen, but she was glad that I was not nineteen. And I that I had cooled off. It was about time to go to the apartment.

    I walked to the convivence store, cutting through side streets, seeing as much as I could along the way, grand structures, brick and stone, steel and iron, concrete forming foundations, among a vast network of thoroughfares and glowing curtain walls branching off throughout the island, sort of as I had studied development in Portland and Boston, San Diego and Los Angeles. The original infrastructure preserved the contrast of creation between stages of development. I had gone on the cobblestone streets and walkways in Portland, and I thought of the two dolphins made of granite right in the middle of the street, a small vestige of colonial times. Between Market and Exchange, inlaid stones and slabs of granite accompanied old brick buildings. The sensation of mist appeared on the extremities as a breeze carried inland some fog from the sea. The setting was opaque with condensation and then at once the sun came out and a spectrum of light formed in the sky above the bay. Hopping from stone in the road to the road made of stone, the seabirds waddled and sounded overhead as the iron bell rung. The smell tidal and floral permeated and combined with that of dinnertime, exciting the birds, and it is evocative. At the apartment, Philbrook must in a quarrel, the sound of a plate shattered and the shout of man came through. Down on the stoop two girls had just smoked cannabis and one tripped on the sidewalk before going upstairs. In New York, at the convenience store, the proprietors I had left my bags with were not there and then my suitcase and backpack could not be found. Until another customer stepped up and asked for her bag, and when she was handed the bag, she said that it was not her bag. It was my backpack. She gave it to me, and at that time the manager came up from the basement with my suitcase and handed it to me. I said thanks and then went outside.

    At the apartment on Suffolk, Miley finished making my bed just as I knocked on the door. She had been in the apartment for a little while, and she liked it. Her friends did too. She had lived in Boston, the neighborhood Beacon Hill on the peninsula, almost directly across from the Boston Commons and adjacent to Acorn Street, the narrow way made of classical cobblestones. I had first walked that passageway as a young boy and each stone placed on the walkway grabbed my attention. She really enjoyed the proximity to the city center. I was near streets made of cobblestone, I told her, but not cobblestones like on Acorn Street. But there was the bay, the beach a little way away, many restaurants, bars, shops, stores, museums, and maybe go for a sail, or even take a ferry to an island. Excuse me. "I'm going to take a shower," I said.

"Of course, towels are in the closet and help yourself to anything in the fridge. Do you want a glass of water?"

"Yes, please. Perfect."

I drank it down. I gestured to the kitchen counter.

"Just put it in there. Anywhere is fine."

That night I ate ramen on a patio behind the building. Along the brick walls there were plants and sculptures and vines and lights strung around, and I washed everything down with a carafe of sake and then I went for a walk. At one point, though I hadn't crossed the river, I thought that I was in New Jersey, Hoboken maybe, or Jersey City. On the other side of the river that I was on high-rises were going up. I looped around. The moon sat over the city, reflecting a gradience of light from the highest point down, and in that dim radiance I got back on Suffolk and went to the apartment. In the morning, I woke up to sunlight coming through the windows, onto the bedding and pillows, like golden wavy hair. I then set off for Midtown. When I arrived in the morning, the sun seemed to shine down directly overhead, a hot sun, and a humid morning. I went along the roadways, between blocks of shade cast from structure to structure, agency to publisher. I drank lemon water at the counter, refreshing the adventure. Back on Broadway each ray of refracted light seemed to penetrate even the ground. The subway whirred and rolled below. I rose up with the sun upon the next stop. I did a slow walk, another mile. There are many people in the street, around the corner and across the city there are many more streets, structures, performances. There was a man in a masquerade mask, and men and women alike gazed at him in awe, still in the dim light of last night. I move past the crowd and finally get to another, filtering in and out, in Time Square. Among thousands of people, Oceane may be one. And she was one, in over a million. I remember that while writing I anticipated an advancement of consciousness. Is it not expanding in in time and space? But to a more defined, contrastive form, just as the night longs to be day, the sun to set, the ocean to swell, the tide to ebb; as a seed is to a sprout, a leaf to a tree, a bird to the sky. How easy the errands, Ocean, if one had wings! I walked to the Empire State Building from 5th Avenue and stood atop the observation deck. With the blue sky as the backdrop, the horizon sat level to me, and structures in view overlaid its continuity.

Just as I had stood on the cliffs of Point Loma looking out at the broad Pacific, from the eighty-sixth floor of the Empire State Building I looked out toward the horizon, the blue sky between breaks in the clouds, blue water between breaks of land through which rivers flowed and the ocean swelled. All around sprawled a mighty metropolis. From the streets down below, buildings erected on each side and multiplied from the central landmark. Cranes advanced the view, contrasting designs of the past with the new. The pattern from an ariel view remains constant by design. There may be slight progressions in structure, additions in layout, a checkered pattern throughout, cut through by Broadway. Going along the thoroughfare, even its name has inspired many. In every direction stands some of the most progressive architecture in concentration reaching out to the horizon. The structures are immense, intricately planned and refined in design. A simple high-rise oceanside can be extraordinary. With a thirty-story courtyard, how is that possible? Each unit is a two-story dwelling, stacked on top of one another fifteen times and each time offset along a radial pattern, creating the space for a private courtyard every third story so as to give each resident the illusion that they live but slightly elevated above the ground. Meanwhile they might be living on the top floor, with a view level to the horizon opposite their facing direction, likewise on every other floor below. That sensation remains constant. At that point I was in a meditative state, with maybe hundreds of people crammed around the observation deck, some on tours, and hundreds more waiting in line. Miley had said that there was street parking, and though directly below there were no parking spots, maybe I could have found one by the apartment. Instead I went down the elevator, and I walked down 5th Avenue to Washington Square Park and continued along on foot back to the apartment.

Later I got a ride uptown. I sat up front. The driver said that he and his girlfriend were going on a vacation. They were going on a road trip along the Pacific Coast Highway. He was from the islands and had been in America for a few years and wanted to see all of it. That is a beautiful geography to start with, diverse landscapes, cityscapes and seascapes blending aesthetically along its span between extremities. Mountain ranges rise up from the edge of the sea, coastal canyons and bluffs, islands and isles, fog between trees, stretches of beach. There is the colonial history of the Northeast, and are the native histories of the Southwest, landmarks, and vestiges throughout the continent. I was going to a pizzeria. I stepped out and went inside and I ate arancini with olive oil. I drank a glass of wine.

After dinner I met up with a group of people at a bar across the street. They were all college students from around the world, and altogether there were about a dozen of us. The bar was no-frills. Old-time tips covered the brick wall behind the counter, one-dollar bills crinkled with signatures in red. Hard rock played in the background. A few people in the group tried to dance but lost their rhythm, though later that night at a club they found their groove. The spot played a mix of rap, pop, and electronic, and the Europeans got hyped on the dancefloor. Then outside on the roof, Maxi dropped his glass on the floor beside Tina. It broke, and as Maxi stood frozen, a few drops of blood dripped from the side of Tina's sandal. I got a cloth from the bartender and took her into the bathroom to clean up, and her friends followed. I cleaned her foot and sandal fast as the other girls stood by the door. The pace resumed as we stepped out, and each room in the place filled up with patrons, some dancing hard, others light, or mingling, standing, sitting. The door opened to the night. Light shone through windows like stars dotting the space in order, checkered stars, in a vertical order. I later waited below on the sidewalk with Nina, a warm breeze blowing by, carrying a sweet scent.

The next day I went to Central Park. I sat by the large pond with turquois water. Many people walked along the pathway around its edge. A dog appeared eager to go for a swim, gazing intently at the small ripples on the surface of the water. A few clouds floated in the sky and the sun shone down on the oasis. Each structure towering in the foreground glistened. I sat for a moment longer in the shade. Behind the setting a little way, the great lawn was full of people, sitting or sprawled out on the grass, sunbathing, eating, reading, relaxing. The smell of cloves and watercress swept by in the breeze, along with some nostalgia. It was dinner at a landmark. Then in the morning, I took a bus back to the apartment.

Through July, I worked and exercised and I studied at leisure. Part of that was reading, and I suppose I could have written more then, experimenting with other forms and styles. And as I'm in the middle of writing this book, it might seem easier if I had recorded everything in the moment or right after. I jotted down some notes from that weekend in New York on the bus ride back to my apartment, as the grand cluster of structures fell back in the distance, standing as inspiration, and with each turn appeared lower and closer to the horizon. It was a sold-out bus. Just as we were leaving the city, and just as we were driving through Brooklyn, though through the window downtown stood far off and across a river, many skyscrapers in the cluster towered over the surrounding infrastructure like mountains. Under the twelve o'clock sun it was a magnificent sight.

"Excuse me," I said.

"Yes, go ahead."

I scooted in front of the girl next to me and got my backpack from the cubby above, then slid in from the other direction and sat down and took out my laptop. Maybe she was musing, because I was filled with inspiration. I had to write. It felt like a dream for much of the ride. Two days later I hiked a mountain and practically ran to the summit, I was so inspired. I took notes, that the feeling on top of a mountain is like that on top of a monumental building, but it is incomparable. A sense of awe and accomplishment came on top of both. I mused on the bus ride, about a bus ride to Boston with Esme. I was excited, because of the concert that we were going to, feeling even the earth rotating, ever revolving around the sun. The passage from then to the period after finishing my first book was not subtle or brief, it was about half a decade, eventful, painful, special and memorable, all in a recent day. Yet the memory on the bus rose to the top of consciousness and sprouted. Becoming more vivid and vibrant, it flowed out onto the page.

I saw her afterward downtown, or at least I thought that it was her, on a bright afternoon right before going to San Diego. I was going on an evening walk. As I stepped outside, I thought, Ashley's in town, and I thought of seeing her, and then I did. I had not been in touch with her since the concert in Boston, and it was not until I had been in San Diego for about a month that I wrote her a letter which I never sent. It started with Pacific Beach, the aesthetic of the city. I added that I like to write and had been writing a bit. A lot had happened since those times on the mountain, and it was good to see you. Maybe you were wearing a sun dress, a floral skirt? There was more to my writing, under a layer of consciousness, a brief but dense letter written quickly.

That July, before clearly understanding my abdominal pain, the connection between the digestive system and the central nervous system, and the interconnection of every bodily system under the microbiome. It is a nexus for microbiota. I ate a lot of fruit and ran daily the greatest trail in the woods to exercise off the excess sugar stored from that fruit. There was fresh and dried fruit. All combined, its nutrient profile was like that of candy. The running trail was just about five minutes away, carved along the wooded floor, between trees and over mounds, hugging the river's edge. I used to tell Ryan that the city was built in a jungle, if the climate were tropical year-round, not only in the summer. If those deciduous trees and plants had not entered dormancy each year, especially the ferns and weeds on the forest floor, they might now be enormous. The trail followed a river, for the most part, straight to its mouth. And then to the sea. When water levels were high, and they almost always were, its rapids flowed over and surged down rocks and ledges. People brought tubes and drifted along the river before the roar of the falls. I thought of documenting the trail running, syncing to each video the music that I listened to in real time, which were instrumentals of jazz or on the guitar, and then compiling them together. On those runs, I timed every step, stride and stop to sync with the songs in a sort of adroit manner. Similarly, that must have unconsciously influenced the book that I was working on, carrying out each step, writing, editing and refining in an equal, sort of adroit manner. The energy exerted is somewhat inexplicable, spontaneous, impromptu. It may be relative to the energy consumed, converted to inspiration, all through the bodily systems.

Earlier that month my roommate from college visited me. We saw the river along which I ran but from its widest section on another prominence of land. My other roommate had come in the afternoon, and we saw some parts of downtown and around the apartment. Not long after that, I met a group of people who had grown up with him. It was at a tropical night out. That was the theme, and they wore floral shirts. They were celebrating the groom's marriage. We went to restaurants, bars and venues throughout the hot spot of the night, and then the groom and most of the group went to a club a little way away. I brought the others to a late-night cafe for snacks. I drank water and ate light.

About halfway through August, right before I started working at the store, I began rewriting and refining my first book. I was diligent through the end of the month. My pace picked up again after meeting Hannah and then subsequently Ana. And it already had, trying to complete as much as I could before the literary agents came to the library and I went in to pitch the book.

Zach and his girlfriend came by at the end of the month. He saw my crystal ball from the entryway. Said it looked nice. The library was getting excited for the start of fall. Asked how everything was going at the store. It was going well, and I was beginning to get a better understanding of the gastrointestinal system. A foundation of information formed, ingredients on labels stored in memory, which later emerged and came to mind while deciphering the digestive disorder that I figured out after the start of this book, the foods, beverages and substances that trigger it and its distress within the body and mind. What a painful period that was. Writing that book amid that distress illustrated in a way the connection between both bodily systems.

On the very first day I learned a set of codes. They said to remember them because after orientation everyone is quizzed. I forget all but one of the codes. Satisfy and delight the customer, that was it. On that first day, I assisted many customers and even the team leader, who somewhat reminded me of Kyle, or vice versa when I saw Kyle the following summer. From then until about the end of the month I got accustomed to the new schedule, the increased workload in regard to my book, courses, and work. Trying to finish that version as fast as possible, I was at it full time and for all three. Although I worked overtime on the book, I was quite focused and attentive throughout the day. My mother did not understand how I was simultaneously working, going to school, and writing a book. After the ordeal, I had amazed myself with the recovery. This period of hyperactivity in a way was about a year after that. I was twenty-two. Each morning was overwhelming. I wrote deep into the night. The microorganisms in my body were imbalanced then, and my good microbiota must have been distressed, signaling a stress response to the central nervous system. It was nearly constant for that period and others. With refinement, I thought, hopefully they will think that my book is better. But I realized not until the following rewrite, the previous two were drafts, and that I will think that it is better.

I spent a lot of energy reworking my first book, often in intervals throughout the day, in the morning, between classes, coursework and study, and then for a longer period into the night after working at the store until ten. It was unbelievable, the motivation for all that. I studied as much as I could. I went to the store preparing to write after. Each department at the store had its own team and the members of each team were acquainted and worked with one another. There was Sophia and she was on one of the other teams. She may have been in college, and I thought that she was cute. One weekend I ran into Brian on my team in the Boston Commons. It was nearing the start of fall and the sunlight casting down on the open space and buildings all around began to grow lighter and fainter, but the leaves on trees and the landscape were still green and appeared verdant in the afternoon light. The eloquent swan swam behind Brian.

"What's up, dude! Just casually seeing another team member in the Commons."

"Brian?" I said. "Yes!"

"Hell yeah! I'm staying in Allapattah and seeing some of the landmarks."

"Boston is an awesome city."

He had seen a lot of the historical landmarks around downtown earlier that day. As a boy I was fascinated by them, and the science exhibitions, the aquarium.

"I'm going to prepare to pitch."

"I hope soon dude. It's getting dark out."

"It is soon but I'm just preparing to pitch my book. I'm going to the Bukowski Tavern. It's for the charm."

"Bukowski! Hey, that's fun. I'll see you next week?"

"See you next week."

Brian went off toward the harbor, the narrow streets shadowed between some of the earliest walls and facades of the city.

Going into pitch my book at the library, I was confident that I was going to work with a literary agent. I had already written the book and was further refining it. I thought that the pitch went well, but she insisted that I write a formal book proposal. I started working on that the next day.

I told Sophia that I was writing a lot. I'm working on a proposal right now—well. I was working hard on that proposal, more diligently than on the book, and at the better intervals throughout the day. Some of the longer, open periods in the day were dedicated to the proposal. My pace picked up. My book too was flowing. How's it going? There were all these other phenomena orbiting the world, condensation, currents, magnetism, mist. I digressed. That was concurrent with its absorption of energy. On a sunny autumn afternoon, I went out for tea. And toward the middle of the month, I made plans to see Ana in Boston.

She was from Brazil, and she had been traveling around America for the past month with her sister and her aunt. Before that they had gone to Canada and saw Toronto, spent a week in Montreal, and then traveled to the Green Mountains of Vermont and New Hampshire. They went through Maine along the coast to Acadia National Park. I told her that they went to New England at the right time of year and she asked because of the leaves? They were lovely. They had gone to the top of a mountain, and her sister looked out and thought that the view of the forest and the ocean in the foreground was like a painting, because the leaves had such radiant colors, shades of the sunset, red, yellow, and orange. She liked to go mwah, with that elusive accent, *mwah*. She and her sister traveled to Portland. That was when we first started talking. They shopped and explored a bit before going to Boston. The following two days we stayed in touch, and then I had two days off.

I texted her before she left, as she left and as she was on her way. I was doing it her way, anticipating that writing a book proposal will get me to the publisher faster, my book published traditionally, and then a smoother, more assured start on the next one. A serene start. But a book proposal for roman a clef might be unusual, especially stream of consciousness, but I completed it. It was a lot of extra work, and I mentioned that to Ana, that I had been busy and then had two days off. I remember telling her about it around ten at night and I had asked about leaving early. Ana had a lot planned for the morrow, and if I came to her in the afternoon, she needed to be refreshed and well rested.

I went to see her the next day in the afternoon. I was somewhat unnerved because of the weather, the drizzle that turned to rain, the clouded sky and fog almost denser than mist. Moisture was in the air, and so were rays of light, because in just minutes the sun dissipated the clouds and its radiance filled the space. All the way into the city its glow streamed through the window, and then from South Station I walked through Chinatown and past the theaters to Ana's hotel. Her sister was inside. I left my backpack in her room and then we went outside. We walked on the sidewalk by Back Bay and went through the Commons, watching the swans, the pale birds, elegant creatures. The squirrels were frolicking. I told her that someone had seen a deer in the Commons. Imagined that after a snowstorm, antlers down, grazing the blanketed meadow. A wild deer trotting into the city and prancing around right in the middle of it. "Hey," she said. "Look. The swans, yes! Hold my hand, Andrew. What is that, those bricks?"

"That's the Freedom Trail," I said.

"The Freedom Trail. Come on, let's follow it."

And we did. Together we went along the pathway. The autumn wind reddened her cheeks. Perhaps women of the colonies went the same way, with hair as red as the sunset, in the candlelight on a setting of cobblestones. In an everchanging realm of progressive technology, communication, fashion, the present unrolls from the past and innovations gather in the current, winding in course like a river, the stillness of water in continuous motion. There are rapids, sediment and sentiments, minerals, flora and fauna, the sun, the moon's pull. Ana was a moon, and she pulled me along the pathway. In the present, for the moment, we're hand in hand.

All the wind and the walking made Ana hungry. Portuguese was her native language. She had learned English well before her trip to North America. Earlier the sisters had gone to Harvard and toured the square and courtyards. M.I.T. sat facing the sunrise positioned at the forefront of the Charles River. We were walking along the Freedom Trail, marked by inlaid bricks along the pavement connecting many of the landmarks, the historical structures, meeting places, points of interest integral to the American Revolution in one course. Then we veered off the trail and stepped into a bar for snacks and a drink. We sat at a table off to the side and opposite the counter. Seats were filling up. Patrons drifted in through the door with the breeze. I am very self-possessed at this time of day, she said. One half makes the other half whole. Consciousness rolls out like a wave, making way down the middle and symmetrical. What is decoded in one mind and the other may be very different or very similar. It can be like something lost in translation. If a paper is written in English and translated into Portuguese for Ana to study, and then that same paper is translated back into English, some of it may be lost or even completely different from translation. We sat relaxed at the bar, at the thick wood table by the front window. We finished the hors d'oeuvres, and then we paid and left. We stopped at the store on the walk back to the hotel.

Ana held up a bottle of wine. "Mwah, mwah," she went, kissing the air.

"Do you want to get anything else?"

We got a bottle opener checking out. "All right. Let's go to your place."

"To the rooftop?"

"We can take the stairs."

"The stairs! You know, in Brazil, I go to the gym. On the trip, not once! Tsk-tsk."

"That's all right."

"The girls in Brazil all go to the gym and they all have nice glutes."

"You do too."

Back at the hotel we climbed the stairs up to her room. "Wait out here," she said. "My sister's inside. One minute, I just have to get my blanket."

I waited in the hall for a moment, and then we went up to the rooftop. It appeared to be closing down for winter. The lights were dimmed and no guests were on the deck. The brightest light came from the crescent moon and spots from the streets below and the windows on buildings in every direction. A few leaves slid along the floor but there were no trees around. Unless there had been trees outside in pots, then were brought inside at the change of season. In the summer, the rooftop spot must be popular, I thought. There were lounge chairs and benches and tables all around the space and in the center was a walk-up bar closed for the evening. Perhaps in the summer there were cabanas too, curtained spaces in which tables and chairs with cushions were set, and dining, and somehow, some kind of water feature or grotto, easily disassembled for the winter and reassembled for the summer. There was a freshwater grotto near Ana's home in Brazil, entering from a cave in waist-deep water sits a deep pool of warm turquois water enclosed by rocks on every side but one through which a light current flows and a few plants grow between rocks in the walls and down the opening where the only sunlight streams through and it is when the sun is shining directly above. We had taken a spot on the padded bench, and between sips of wine, we began to digress, discovering fantasies, reveries, dreams, ideas, insights, ambitions. It was more than I thought, I recalled. She spoke with a subtle, soft accent. There was moist dew under the light of the moon. She said, "You're a writer, yes. Well, write about me."

From the sound of doves through her window and possibly a great bird in the sky or perched on rocks above the grotto, soon after sunrise, she calmly rises ready to go. When she opens her eyes she searches her mind preparing for the day ahead, almost like the great bird in the sky, dreamily surveying the terrain below. Go forward, up, down, slowly, slowly, and then she's off, never once flying the field in circles, composed in form, emitting her light as though from within.

She dreamt of going from law into politics, after completing her studies, and I of writing a book. But that was a dream underway. To write in a big space connected with nature, plants, foliage, from the exterior to the interior, airflow carrying scents of patchouli, lavender, sandalwood, the sound of trickling water, the circulation of light and energy, a palpable fengshui highlighting the way to fantasy. She can take off for the stars, if the stars are in proper alignment, and fly beyond the atmosphere to a parallel sphere, symmetrical along every axis, every rotation presenting a unique view of the distinct world to which she flew. Then we kissed, and the night became bright under her light, and delicate. Even each motion was passionate, each detail lost, as each's own light reflected back and formed a whole.

"This is nice." She laughed. "You're just like *Ana this is nice. This is the American lust!*"

"You're right," I said.

"Yes."

"And you're bright."

"Mwah, you're funny."

"Am I spending the night?"

"Yes, but my sister…"

"I don't mind."

"She won't either. But, ugh. She's my younger sister. She has a good nose. You will come see me tomorrow, yes. Come. Stay the night. We will stay at your place."

"Yes."

"Mwah, mwah."

I finished the proposal after the first time seeing her, thirty pages with chapter summaries, and then I sent it to the literary agent. When I was asked to write a book proposal, I realized that doing one might be unusual for roman a clef, stream-of-consciousness books. The book was unrefined then, and it streamed fast for a first book despite that distress through which it was written. But I went through with the book proposal, and then I continued working on the revisions. I had pursued a book deal and had ambitions of creating more books. Ana and I met up the following afternoon. And through the evening streets and walkways, as the sun fell behind buildings, then trees, then earth, with the sunset around each turn, we went to the marketplace. We ate dinner, and then we went in for the night.

After getting back to my apartment, I began reworking the book again. Before pitching it, I had gone through the book once, made some modifications, but mostly added more details and essentially more to its outline instead of editing sentences and structure. I wrote not exclusively about the book, or rewriting the book, but recorded bits and pieces of the experiences, musings, meditations while working on it. While in the mind everything is fresh, it is fastened to the foundation of an unrolling consciousness. I went to school in the afternoon. Excited, I was in a somersault seeing Hannah in the cafe. It was right after catching up with Elias in the lobby. He had a strong accent, as though speaking out of the corner of the mouth. Hannah was sort of testy, and she sounded exquisite. She had a unique frequency. It was light, girlish. I was completely tuned into the moment. Elias had mentioned that he was working on a paper that was due at the end of the hour. He wanted to open a gyro joint downtown, because it's a bustling area that needs authentic Greek cuisine. I said that I liked Greek food. He asked about getting a bite to eat, but I was busy. "Come on," he said. "You're writing, right? How is it?"

"All right," I said. "More than I thought. What makes it different is the cloud cover."

"You can't judge a book by its cover."

"No."

"In the stores on display. Hold on, no I remember one in New York, the one by Central Park, my wife took me inside. Bro there were like massage tables in the middle of the store and people were getting massages. Yeah, I got one. They gave samples and it's a massage!" He dabbed my arm. "No you know what. Pretty soon they'll have movie theaters in there right in the middle of the store, a big screen and chairs, make the popcorn too."

"Yes, that could be Amazon's initiative. They're even a big publishing house."

"Publishing. Then there's Prime."
"Yes. Anyway, I have to get back to this paper. I'm finishing it up right now."

And then moments later I finished the paper and got up and went down the hall to the cafe. I made a coffee and added some sugar and stirred and there was Hannah. She had a canvas with her. I thought that she must create unique art. "Do you want my number?" she asked.

"Yeah," I said.

Inspired, ideas flowed through my mind all afternoon. And then there's Ana and then there's Elias and then there's work and then there's the book and all the while there's Hannah. She has a unique last name, and I wondered is it Italian? Apparently everyone thought she's Italian, but actually, Puerto Rican! We texted and I learned that in class. The next day passed and everything appeared clear, the morning light of the sun, the moon she shone from, and soon my mind eased, engaged in the afternoon date that Hannah and I had set. Getting ready with her friends, seeing if we're still on for tea at five, and where is it again?

I sat waiting at the table, responding to her updates. Sorry I'm running late, the traffic's bad, but I found a spot. It was at a booth. Then she walked through the door with two of her friends. She had on a sweater and leggings and before sitting down she grave a light flick of the wrist. "How are you!" she said. "These are my friends. This is Sadie and this is Leigh."

Sadie was from Vermont, Hannah told me, and Leigh was raised by the beach. Leigh had beach blonde hair, and Hannah's was dark, and Sadie had a mix of both.

"What about you," I asked. "Puerto Rico?"

"No," she laughed. "Do I look Puerto Rican?"

"She looks cute," said Sadie, "Doesn't she?"

"Yeah," said Leigh.

"Yeah."

"Right now I live in the dorms," Hannah said. "We all live in the dorms. Sadie and Leigh are roommates and I live right down the hall. Basically I have the place to myself. My roommate's only there three days a week. Let's see, Tuesdays, Wednesdays, Thursdays.

She's tidy and then she takes her stuff and leaves, so we all hang out in my room. Wanna see it?"

She showed me a picture.

"Nice. That's a suite."

"Where do you live?" she asked.

"Just a couple minutes away. My apartment's in the Wadsworth."

"That's cool."

"It's right back there actually."

"What the address?"

I told her, and then she got on her phone and checked it out on maps. Sadie smiled, and then she said, "Oh, she's already stalking you."

"I was just seeing if we're close by it."

Hannah and I planned to meet up on the weekend. She decided on Saturday, and I had the day to get together with her. I had told Jane in leadership that I met a girl and have been thinking about her. On Saturday, Hannah slept in, and she was going to tell me about her morning and last night when we get together. Just give her an hour or two to get ready. And then she was off. She fixed her hair back and let it fall down to her shoulders. An hour passed, and then two. At the tearoom she was magical. A lot of things were cute to her, the hostess, her pants, the menu, art, table and cups. The interior was too. The menu for tea was thick and formatted like a chapter book. The blends we ordered came in teapots. I poured her a cup. She had a sip and was back in her element. She talked about her time in New York with her friend.

"She's an artist," she said. "She's a silent pianist. She sits at the piano and that's all." A piano was playing in the background. It must have been part of the ambient soundscape inside. Pianos are good décor. I like the sound of a symphony. Hannah liked my tea.

"So what happened last night?" I asked.

She was downtown with Sadie and Leigh, and she was going to let me know. They had some cannabis. Just a little bit. She didn't often, but she and the other girls had an urge to have some. She was going to see if I wanted to meet them by the square. They were walking around, and they were high, setting with the sun, falling for the moon.

"The place with chili pepper lights inside, what is that?"

"It's a restaurant, one of favorites actually."

Well, when she saw the pepper lights inside, she flashed the pepper lights from outside. And it was crowded. I wished that I had been inside. I drank my tea.

"I'm hungry," she said.

"Let's get something to eat."

Later she asked if I wanted a ride to my place. She wanted to see which building was mine. It was next to The Dutch Door. They served breakfast brunch and lunch. I thought, she might have liked The Dutch Door, for brunch. The book was in its refining stage. She pulled out of her parking spot. I told her where to turn, when to slow down, keep going, right there. She pulled over to the side of the street and parked. It was the afternoon. She got a spot up front. I went to work on the book.

And I worked on the book whenever I had the chance to. I remember the passion that I had for writing that book. Part of that passion came from a promise I made to someone that I had written to, a celebrity; that I was going to write a better book than the first one. I worked on it through the night some nights, during intervals between classes, before and after work. I was in the groove, and I hoped that by refining the book I might meet him, query another agent, get into the school of my dreams. I worked thoroughly on every task, and effectively I sometimes worked on the book in my mind without writing anything down. Fine details and notes streamed through my mind, sifting, playing perhaps like the silent pianist, and those on top streamed out through consciousness afterward.

I recall the songs, the duties, the tasks, the stairs and upstairs, the halls, the rooms, the tables, the dinners and after dinner, the coffee from downstairs sometimes. I remember the back hall where a lot of others congregated. Someone might have been trying to stand on both hands in the corner, balancing upside down, leaning against the walls. Maybe Brian strolled through and said, "Hey dude," and then gave the gymnast's leg a little pat before cartwheeling over and standing upright. The other Bryan sometimes wore a kilt, I believe, with a sporran.

The maze went far beyond numbers and letters. In a rhythm I pressed the keys on the keyboard like playing a piano and typed. It was a painstaking symphony. I prepared all day for that, planning to get in that rhythm.

Some days I thought of Sophia. I remember she was at the sink one time, squeezing lemons, oranges, or both, and she made me juice that I should not drink. I got her a set of assorted facemasks for when she sprayed the machine, which was right before Covid-19, before facemasks became part of daily wear during that time.

I recalled the last duty for the night at the store, and that was facing. I thought that for a task it was a way to cool down and unwind, and it was predominantly when I worked on the book in a way, but not writing or editing, rather collecting ideas and information in the sieve of consciousness. Then later that night, after the mind naturally sifted the sieve, some of that streamed out into the book or was added in. It was like facing, in a way. Items were added in or brought from the back of the shelf to the front, two items, upright or upside down, depending on the time of year, the position of the world in relation to the sun. That was facing. As opposed to ideas and information stored in the back of the mind, or else the profound depths of consciousness, and brought to the front through the mind's sieve. Instead of two items, it could have been two million ideas and bits of information being sifted through by natural processes of consciousness at once. It was almost an automatic function, a natural process of the mind that was hyperactive at that time. My digestive system may have been trying to function in unison with it. At times I was in pain. Normally I preferred to formulate and instill new ideas, or to solve problems that are hard to figure out, which is probably why I wrote a lot then and enjoy writing in general. After going into a meditative state of mind, and that could have been from exercising in a fluid manner, a heightened sense of total consciousness formed, and wit flowed through my nearly subconscious mind. I saw early one morning at the time of writing this book the incredible subconscious in action, a part of total consciousness, but fully asleep in a deep dream. It was a strange dream in which I suddenly regained consciousness at a desk sitting before a typewriter. I had flown to the desk, in that overnight dream, a kind of motion completely new to me. I was pressing the keys with only one hand and the sound of the machine was incredible, because I was writing so fast. The fastest one-handed writer, I thought, as I held page after page with my other hand and read to myself what had just streamed out about breakthrough ideas on consciousness, novel to intelligence. It was like reading a new book by a prolific author written with one hand, because two were being written at once, and the two streams converged into a larger river flowing into the estuary of total consciousness.

I went through page after page. I ran out of every blank page on the desk. I was writing on a typewriter machine, but it was like I was the machine: a first-person perspective of total consciousness. I have since lost all that novel work in its tracks, I think, everything that my subconscious was trying to stream out and articulate about consciousness, except for all that recycled back into the mind's sieve. Upon regaining consciousness to the first sunlight of day streaming through the window shades, I recalled the last paragraph, a paragraph written in subconscious thought, because at the turn of consciousness my subconscious mind took a snapshot of that page and presumably the pile of manuscript paper. It was the exercise of a photographic memory, in a way. Written days like this always seem to make the ball drop. Days between, the wheel stop. Wind, passing by like a tight dream. Walking on the sunset to tomorrow. Perception in the present. *Finis*. There was a good line on the last page, almost like a stanza, and there were maybe hundreds of other pages, thousands of other paragraphs, all composed in the subconscious mind, maybe rapidly in dream time, instantly in the moment, and I endeavored its composure in the physical. After all, this writing and that comes from the same mind, subconscious or conscious. That it is part of total consciousness I have no doubt, but whether there is a link or a passageway connecting this, the exertion of potential energy, to total consciousness, is yet undiscovered. Possibly interweaving many realms, medicine, linguistics, physics, math, biology, psychology, architecture, engineering, and all others into a larger domain is part of its natural process, and only recently has that been streamlined through the progression of technology. Subconsciously my mind worked effectively, and simultaneously so did my body; I thought rapidly, and my fingers danced hastily to get it all down. That was at the time of my second book, this book, and sometimes the stream filled completely before flowing from my mind. In that case, I wet my thumb, turned the page and commenced afresh. I recalled the stillness of light wind at the nearby square or else on the wharf at a time of digression. I forgot about myself in the bustle of the setting, among the blend of landscape, cityscape and seascape. At the store, the moment the last task of the day began, my mind began sifting through the stream. I was writing in a way, only not down on a piece of paper. It was sort of a warm-up exercise, because once I was back at the apartment, I worked on the book well into the night. By morning, maybe two or three or four new pages had been composed, and then I went off to class. Often after two, one in the morning and another in the middle of the day, I went to the store in the afternoon. I was almost too preoccupied to think. People chatted while facing. I was studying, meditating, or preparing to channel the energy of the night ahead. I was quiet but attuned to the display. Someone might have thought that it's powerful to have ten billion people on the planet, when only a century ago the population was about one tenth of what it was then, so in a century there could be upwards of fifty or a hundred billion people. There's more than a balance of constant conflict between contraction and expansion. I thought, that could be the horsepower behind consciousness, and it too experiences exponential growth, expanding and contracting in alignment with the universe. Theory on consciousness commenced. Conceived sometime around then, related notions on that and innatism had been sifting through and cycling back into the mind well beforehand.

Arthur was a young man with sunset hair. A burly man who at first I had mistaken for Tim from the library approached Arthur for assistance with an item, and with pleasure Arthur helped him. He satisfied and delighted Tim, and then Tim thanked Arthur with a big hug and a few pats on the back. "The funniest thing just happened," said Arthur. "We saw, Art," said Brian. "You're a lovable person." Then I regained focus back in consciousness. The moment we all finished, I went to the Wad, up the hill and south down the avenue. Sometimes there were great flashing lights from an ambulance or police car turning the corner or an event going on by the civic center. Other times heading back to the Wad, I walked through the sunshine, the moonlight, the rain or snow, but nothing compared to the snowstorm that I walked through on my way to South Station. It was a blizzard, totally whiteout conditions. What should have been a ten-minute walk took about an hour at the most and I missed the bus. It was a winter wonderland, as big snowstorms are sometimes called. To someone or something looking down below from above, perhaps God, a higher energy, a supreme consciousness, it must have seemed like a snow globe. The wind, the lights, the icicles and snow; incredible. The following week Mark said, "Quite the storm, huh?" and I told him that I had walked right through the middle of it. He had lived in Boston, in the heart of downtown. The building that he had lived in had quite a few characters, he said. Many were college students. There was someone at his door one time, and then he went to open it. "'Hey,' I said. "'Curly, right?' Yeah—yes. Curly, yep. Thought I was a professor."

"Were you?"

"I did philosophy."

"Philosophers like consciousness, debates on domains alike."

It was the holiday season, from November to January, and I recalled the store bustling with activity and patrons getting jammed up back to the lobster tank. A glass bottle drops and the symphony begins. The jingle bells jingled and the sound of chimes rang in. Then in the morning, I went to class, and depending on the day I had a couple of classes, and then I went to the store straight from class, and after completing the daily tasks, I went to the apartment and worked more on the book. Those were long days, and weekends were too. I was inwardly exhausted but ambitious and earnest enough to write wholeheartedly through that demanding period. My book, I had mentioned to someone, will be finished by Christmas. I tried to get it right and exceed his expectations for a literary project, in light of the ordeal, injuries, and distress sustained then. As one that was basically written on an enhanced typewriter, that must factor in. There was not any researching or looking up information; it has all come from within, or from the course through which consciousness streams and is then written, almost subconsciously.

I had set the deadline for Christmas and mentioned that it will be finished by Christmas. I worked all night on Christmas Eve just to try and fix every typo and make every sentence roll easily and fit the page perfectly—even though typography on a formatted word document does not always sync perfectly when printing, and the text on the printed page may be spaced a bit differently to fit its margins compared to the electronic document—thinks the typographic wizard.

I drank canned coffee thinking about the company's founder, living in France, staying on a wooden skiff, trying to create the perfect latte. At the same time, I tried to do in one day what might usually take an editorial wizard many, and of all days on Christmas

Eve. After going late into the night, my book was published in the morning.

Creating the book both the first and the second time exhausted my mind. It had to decompress. I rested after Christmas, as I had planned to. I slept through the night, then finished editing the book before New Year's Eve. I recalled working on the second version of the book, and even the first, as though it was that extraordinary dream of the fastest one-handed typer. One night I dreamt of mysticism, then a kind of eroticism, and the energies picked up within.

On New Year's Eve, I saw the entire firework display and holiday performance. And on the night of that dream, I thought about how I then missed the bus by six seconds. I was just about a stride behind almost all the times getting on without breaking a stride. I counted one to six, after the bus was pulling out and before I made it to its parked spot. I went inside the bus station and sat down. I had waited for the light to run its cycle and then I crossed the street, and there had been a parade going on and an elaborate display of fireworks and the sauntering crowd of people and the long march of each member in the band and I stopped time after time to see the night sky and the firework lights and colors and the structures all illuminated, and as the number 20 lit up in the background on the upper windows of a distant building to reflect the start of 2020, I saw the grand finale and marveled at the view of the city but missed the bus by a tenth of a minute.

Meanwhile, Hannah had traveled to Cuba and was maybe at one of the beaches, making grand formations and cairns with rocks in the sand. I hadn't seen her since having the goal of finishing the book by Christmas. I told her that I had finished writing it. She had since gotten back, and I said that I will come to her and show her my book. That was about two hours away. She said that she was going to be back in town the next week, and we waited to get together until then.

In the meantime, I started the next writing project. I tried to keep my mind sharp and feeling fresh, I wrote in an air of stream of consciousness fashion. The momentum continued, and it carried through cognition.

Then I went to a spa, with massage tables and a locker room that had marble floors. Greater profundity came almost right after as soon as I boarded the sensory deprivation tank. Closing the door to the pod, the noise sounded suctional, extraterrestrial, as though part of a space shuttle. The moment the door closed the inside was sort of vacuum sealed and perhaps no outside noise could penetrate through the walls of the tank. The depth of water in which I lay must have been about eight inches. But it felt like I was in a cosmic ocean, floating atop the saline water, a sensation of weightlessness and zero gravity cocooned me. Once my mind stilled, hoisted in body and lightly afloat, I saw what might be in outer space. God, I thought. It must be. What a sudden, obscurely incandescent sensation I had when water seeped into my eyes. Then there was a big splash of water and the taste of the tears of a heart on fire. Later I thought of that entire session and experience as not only good but also enlightening. That night my subconscious revamped. I recalled the visuals of civilizations under oceans, in megacities, on planets, underground, in the sky, floating by, operandi, agendas, foundations, formations of an ever-expanding sphere in space. It was like the sensory deprivation tank. There was one part of consciousness from outside the system, and one part from within.

She liked the cover of the book. Thought that it was vintage, in a way. Sadie was supposed to go to Cuba but her friend went instead and stayed inside or was on the phone the entire time basically. She traveled, saw attractions and landscapes, cityscapes and local cultures mostly on her own. She must be brave, I thought. She wanted to see Europe too, and Australia. At that point she was enjoying her tan. In the spring and in the fall, she could be right-side up or upside-down, depending on the hemisphere. At the same time? It may depend on the position of the sun, the dimensions in space.

She had a bag of clothes with her and needed to return them. That was the first stop we made on the way to my apartment. We returned her clothes, and after making another stop at the library for her textbook, we went inside.

She liked it, and she said that the apartment was like her friend's in New York. I had parked in the garage across the street. She could see it from the window beyond which lay a view of the bay behind some buildings and before the landscape blended with distant hills. In the spring and summer that part of the land was green and then in the fall it transitioned to vibrant foliage. Could set up an easel and paint. That was where I wrote some of the time. The windowsill was big enough to be a desk. She thought that it must be good for some inspiration.

I felt strong emotions that day. The outward incandescence of the moon was vivid and light at night.

The following week I saw Hannah a few times. She was the moon in the daytime sky. I was waiting for my class to start in the lobby of a building, and then she came in and walked over with sails spread and smiling she said, "Are you following me?"

"Or you me?" I said.

Follow the stars, I thought, inward toward the heart. She sat down in my chair and then scooted in. I wrote that I had been good at math, and then she suddenly needed help with her math assignment. I showed her how to do the problems, the steps and patterns. We worked on those in the same chair. It refreshed that part of my mind after having shifted toward literature.

Covid-19 cropped up the following month. The pandemic began, and likewise the movement of matter did too. One came before the other, and the latter had been in the works first, as though through causality.

Then online operations commenced, and there was an opportunity to rework the book without setting a tight deadline for one of the instituters. I had a semester to revise my book, with a greater sense of attention dedicated to it than the previous two drafts. That was my last semester before graduation, and there were a couple of months to try and finish it with more intervals of mostly undivided attention.

This book was different to write. I enjoyed it even with digestive disorders beyond comprehension at that time. New ideas were formed and I tried a new style. In a way, it is stream of consciousness in reverse, my mind on a tangent, consciousness in stream. The metaphysical phenomenon carried on, the star in position, and I wrote in its direction.

It was from ambition and passion that I finished strong my first book, the first and second version, or the revision, and then I wrote about it in this book. Before I had written to him, and before I had started writing the first version of the book, that's when the idea of writing one fell into place. I remembered going to the beach at the time of commencing that endeavor. Sunlight streamed in through the windows, and the sky was clear. It was a day when not only the sun shines, the moon glows.

I was thinking of the dreamy feeling I get by the ocean.

Suddenly a wave breaks, and it has an exciting sound.

And then I worked tirelessly on my first book.

I was twenty-one when I wrote it; nineteen and then twenty, recovering from and navigating through that ordeal.

This book had been developing since before starting the first one. Some of it was written in one stream of consciousness, some in another, and the rest was written and put together in a hurry.